Wak(

In Co.

Women's Prosperity Network

Presents

Conversations
That Make a Difference

Stories Supporting
A Bigger Vision

Parker House Publishing
www.ParkerHouseBooks.com

Foreword

Nancy Matthews
Founder of Women's Prosperity Network

Conversation is defined in the dictionary as an "oral exchange of sentiments, observations, opinions or ideas" and today more than ever due to the speed with which conversations can travel around the world, conversations are having the greatest impact on society.

It is through conversation, the expression and exchange of ideas, that great feats are achieved, inventions conceived and created, love is expanded and humankind evolves. It is also through conversation that misunderstandings occur, emotions are evoked that lead to hurt, anger and disappointment. The quality of our lives and the lives of the people around us and in our world are directly related to the types of conversations we are having – the conversations that are given the most attention.

Women's Prosperity Network and Wake Up Women have joined forces to create *Conversations That Make A Difference* with the intention of creating more conversations that inspire cooperation, collaboration, understanding and love.

It is through this type of conversation that this project came to be. A conversation that I had in 2008 with our editor, Teresa Velardi, where I shared the vision and mission of Women's Prosperity Network (WPN) and she shared her passion to empower women. A conversation between a member of WPN and Karen Mayfield, founder of Wake Up

Women, where Karen and I were introduced. A conversation between Karen Mayfield and our publisher, Candi Parker, where Candi was introduced to WPN. A conversation and an inspired idea between Teresa Velardi and Karen Mayfield to collaborate with WPN to create the space for more women to share their conversations that make a difference.

Each of the authors have shared their insights, stories, passions and their expertise with the intention of giving you, the reader, food for thought and a spark to have your own conversations that make a difference. We know that by encouraging and sharing conversations that make a positive difference in our lives, we will each individually and collectively create a culture that makes a difference.

A culture committed to having conversations that create understanding and support the evolution of humankind by expanding love and compassion.

*"It always seems impossible
until it's done."*

~ Nelson Mandela

Table of Contents

In The Beginning There Was the Word

Karen Mayfield

When we are born, the other humans in our life stimulate the law of curiosity surrounding what will be the first word we will speak. Will it be "Mama"," Dada", "Nana", "Poppa", "Hey", "Hi", "Bye" or some other word that is just ours. Whatever our first word may be, that word is written down in our baby book and from then on will be the word representing us as a human beginning our conversation with the world. As we grow in our awareness, so will our conversation and one by one word after word our vocabulary increases. Words are the center of our communication, the building blocks of our conversations.

However communication can happen even when no words are spoken. Body language or just a look goes a long way in letting someone know what we are saying without uttering a single word. Our verbal conversation, however, normally consists of a series of words that are put together to make a point, or share a feeling, or explain a meaning to thoughts we may have. It is in conversations that are conducted between one or more that create new ways of doing things, change the structure of belief, or build upon an already existing process.

Social media has taken casual conversation and made it global, now conversations are being held at lightning speed. Through social media, the world has become a smaller space. Traveling at the speed of a post we can have a conversation with a person on the other side of the planet. We can form lasting friendships, create business collaborations, joint venture with others, and share our heartfelt mission in just a short conversation. In fact, we are so connected to conversation that we continue our quest to reach out and touch someone using words as a means to create communication. We can post a note, or share and share a like, with ease. And... We love it.

By utilizing a social marketing mindset, I am fully committed to having conversations that make a difference. Every word that I speak it is always intended to lead into conversation that will create a space to help another. Using Connect-Working © I am able to connect with other like minded individuals, corporations, or organizations that are centered around making a difference. One word alone may not make a difference but several words connected together and formed into a conversation can lead to making a difference that will be felt from coast to coast.

The stories that are in this book are stories about conversations, and the difference those conversations have made in the lives of others. Our conversations make a difference.

About the Author

Karen Mayfield is the founder of Wake Up Women. She is an author, speaker, metaphysical minister, and spiritual life coach.

Join Karen as she takes you into the world and brand of Wake Up Women while guiding you through your process of waking up to your life of happiness, health & wealth, with peace of mind to live the life you love.

To learn more about Karen visit

www.wakeupwomen.com

Journey to Your Very Best

Cynthia "Sunshine" Lindsay

Groggily, I opened my eyes to the loudly ringing alarm clock. It was morning again, and I didn't feel like getting out of bed...again. Little did I know that today would be the day I would take the first step to changing the rest of my life.

As much as I enjoyed being in my mid 40's (don't we all forget we are 30 until we look in the mirror?), the fact is that I was feeling much older than I should have. I had been careful to keep my skin looking youthful and maintain my looks, but somehow an extra 60 lbs. had become a permanent fixture on my small-framed body over the last 20 years. No wonder I was so tired all the time. I was carrying around the equivalent of 3 large bags of dog food with me everywhere I went. Every time a new diet or exercise program hit the press, I was the first in line to buy the book, read it and try it out. I had been on every weight-loss program known to mankind from "The Cabbage Soup Diet" to walking 12 miles a day, 5 days a week. Sure, I lost a few pounds here and there, but these 60 lbs. seemed to be my weight to bear. I felt hopeless and discouraged after each failed attempt and somewhere along the way I stopped trying to lose the weight. I resigned myself to just grin and bear it. It didn't really matter that much to me, or so I told myself. I was so busy being a wife, a mother, a business owner, the mediator, and the family's emotional support that I never took time for myself. I never thought there was enough time. I am no stranger to Hard Work. I grew up watching my mom and dad work hard for everything we had. I learned from the best, and I was never scared to get my hands dirty. I dove into my work at home as a wife and mother, as well as a business owner managing life's hectic schedules like a well-tuned machine. I looked in the mirror one day and realized I was totally drained emotionally, physically, mentally and spiritually. Why was I constantly fooling myself into the false belief that I was "blissfully happy"? I never realized how my OWN health and happiness, or lack thereof, could impact the rest of my family, especially my children.

Lesson Learned: Sugar coating every aspect of your life doesn't help anything in the long run.

A child's laughter is more powerful than one thinks. Listening to my young children laughing and playing in the next room moved me to tears. I asked myself, "when was the last time I felt that kind of joy? When was the last time I burst out in a hardy laugh?" I couldn't recall. Then one day, it occurred to me that I never laughed at funny situations or circumstances anymore. The child-like joy had been siphoned from my life like a slow leak, leaving me feeling as lifeless and limp as a little rag doll. I had become very serious about everything. This is when the beautiful tapestry I envisioned as my life started unraveling, and fast. Not only was I devastatingly unhappy, I was also probably clinically depressed, though I did not recognize it yet.

Over the next 6 years, what had seemed like the "perfect family" to everyone else, was crumbling around me. Looking back, I see clearly now, what I had been trying to avoid acknowledging for many years. Not only was I in a failing marriage, it was beyond repair, and the only thing that would stop the downward spiral was making a drastic life change. It was time to take my power back.

Lesson Learned: Address issues at hand as quickly as possible to minimize collateral damage.

Fast forward through all of the ensuing endless drama. It was now my time. God spoke to me. He told me to STOP being a victim and START taking action. Every journey is preceded by preparation. My first step was to hire a personal trainer and become a member at a gym. For the next six months, I would be focusing on my outer body's physical transformation. Each day I got stronger and though I looked and felt much better, weight was not falling off the way I imagined it would. However, my energy levels started to rise and I began to feel better about myself.

Lesson Learned: You are responsible for your life and overcoming the obstacles that are in your way.

Now that I was stronger and feeling more fit, it was time for me to release the material baggage I had been holding onto. Living in a large 5 bedroom house with one child who would be the last to leave the nest, I started thinking about what life would be like when he went away to college. Of all the things we accumulate and place value on, our household and personal effects hold a lot of emotional attachment. They represented love to me. The picture painted for me in a child's art class, the tote bag with photo transfers of bygone days tenderly placed on it, a loving poem written in English class. I didn't have the time or the energy to sift through every item and organize it the way I would have liked to. God hit me with an epiphany that I should sell everything I did not need and move somewhere more suited to my needs; somewhere that I would be able to release the past, reflect on my dreams for the future and live into them. It took about a year of yard sales, Craigslist ads and trips to the local charity, but finally the day came when the moving van was packed and I was on my way to my new home on the beach in Florida. There's something very cleansing and calming about being near the ocean.

Lesson Learned: Starting over is very freeing.

Over the next 2 years, I would be consciously and intentionally rediscovering and redefining myself. At the time of my divorce, I couldn't even tell you what kind of foods I enjoyed or what my favorite color was. Everything in my life had been put aside for another's happiness. I would soon discover who I really was, what I liked and what I wanted for my future. This is when I learned that emotional baggage keeps us enslaved as much as the physical possessions we hold onto. What was done in the past was now over; it could not be corrected or changed. The only thing I had control over was this moment in time and where it would take me. I started loving and caring for myself; something I had let go by the wayside for all too many years. As I began releasing unpleasant memories of the past and the negative patterns that had become such a part of my daily thought process, my emotional state was beginning to heal. Working with many different techniques from meditation and emotional tapping to direct conversations with God, I have been able to restore my emotional wellbeing and finally live out my hopes and dreams.

Lesson learned: Take a chance on your own dreams. The greater the risk... the greater the reward.

As soon as I let my physical and emotional attachments go, I started to focus on the inside of my body by lovingly feeding it nourishing foods. It was at this point that my weight finally started releasing from my body. Happiness took the place of all the physical weight I was holding on to. Slowly, but surely I was becoming a whole person once again. I found that the health of my physical body plays a vital role in having a life full of energy and ease.

As soon as my path of realization became evident, I started working with other people to help them find the highway to their greater selves. This is when I got connected to my power and discovered my true passion in life. I call it my "big why." I use this to teach other's how to define and refine their purpose by igniting a fire under them so that they can connect with the part of them that needs to be healed. As I do this work with others, my own healing continues. It begins first with recognizing the pattern of being "stuck" on life's hamster wheel; going around and around in circles, and never stepping out of the wheel to take hold of all that life has to offer. Sometimes it takes a lot of courage to identify this. It also takes courage to seek change. Because I have travelled this long and grueling journey, my gift to this world is to make the next person's pilgrimage less painful then mine was.

You can begin your quest for an amazing and enlightened life by taking care of yourself emotionally and physically. Feed your mind good self-development meals through reading books written by progressive and positive, forward-thinking authors. Redefine who you are and redirect your life to live into who it is you are truly meant to be. If you could draw a picture of your life and what you would want it to look like, what would that be? Set yourself free to live into your dreams. Then, start taking care of your physical body. Set a goal. Where would you like to see yourself by this time next year? We all end up putting off what we know we need to do. So many people say, "I really need to start eating better", but then never make that a priority. Everything in your life revolves around the foods you are feeding your body. It has an impact on everything you do from how you feel when you wake up in the morning, what you wear, the friends you choose to hang out with, to when you go to sleep and how well you rest....the list is endless. Choose foods that are natural and that grow from the earth. Stay away from anything artificial or genetically modified or engineered. If you would just take the first step of eating nourishing foods that will fuel your body and improve your health, I promise that other areas of your life will fall into place with less effort. Your physical and emotional well-being has a direct impact on all areas of success in your life. Helping other people find happiness through nutritional education so they can improve the quality of their lives, and the lives of their loved ones, is why God put me here on this earth. Having lived through, and claimed victory over that very situation myself, has molded me into the person that I am today. I am extremely grateful for the path I have been shown, through my own long and arduous journey of self-discovery and healing. I am thankful for each and every one of the bumps in the road I have encountered and excited about the future growth I will experience in the next chapter of my life. I've been very good at taking care of everyone else, now it is my time to shine and to help the rest of the world shine as well.

In my work as a Life Coach, Nutritional Specialist and Food Educator I speak to a lot of men and women about their lives, their families, their challenges and inspirations, their self-image, health, and their future dreams. Everyone faces different issues in their lives, but what I've noticed is that in the end, all we really want is to experience peace, love and fulfillment. I would happily tell you that I have all the answers to make your life more meaningful and gratifying, however, we are individually responsible for our own inner work. What I can offer you is education and direction. This journey of life requires that you be an active participant, asking questions and seeking answers that will take you to your destination. Sometimes you have to just grab onto life and say "Hey Buddy, I'm gonna live you to the fullest."

About the Author

Cynthia "Sunshine" Lindsay is a dedicated alternative nutritional specialist, health and wellness coach, speaker. She specializes in the education of others to quickly and elegantly look and feel younger. She serves those in her local community, Palm Beach County, Florida as well as those who connect with her virtually, coaching them to improve their lives.

Sunshine brings extensive knowledge and experience to her busy practice, helping her clients to discover their most direct route to a beautiful life. Her goal is to guide you through current challenges and into a personalized plan for happiness, wellbeing and success.

Connect with Sunshine at: BeautyFarmacy@gmail.com 706.255.8513

Visit her website at http://cynthialindsay.com/

11

"Stay-N-Alive"

Sharise Deimeke

I am so blessed. I am married to the man of my dreams, my high school sweetheart. We have four amazing children who light up my world.

During 2006 I was caring for patients, as I did most days since graduating from Nursing School with a Bachelor's of Science in Nursing. I love people and I really adored my patients with all my heart. I gave them all I had. However, I would often feel empty and unfulfilled living out the daily grind. I often wondered, "Why am I really here?" I had this great tugging in my heart that I was meant to do something else, to become more.

One day, as I was asking the routine questions I asked multiple patients daily in preparation for surgery, I had a random thought. The monotony of the process had begun to take its toll. Anyone could do this job, I even wondered if a monkey could be trained to replace me. Suddenly, I was emotionally stripped wondering if I was providing any value at all to my patients. I thought that anyone could complete these tasks. Logically, I knew this was not entirely the truth; I was educated on how to understand the intricacies of the human body and had acquired skills over the years to accomplish my assessments and necessary treatments. That said, I couldn't help but wonder, "Does anyone else feel like a monkey, going through a series of motions or is it just me?" I found myself feeling dead inside, with my motivation for this profession I had worked towards for so long, gone.

The conversations I have today are so different than the ones I had back then. That was before I became aware that I possessed a desire to be "**alive**". My definition of "alive" is to be fully alive mentally, spiritually, emotionally and physically while I am breathing. I spent fifteen years as a registered nurse at the bedside of many patients conversing with them about their diseases, their failing health and, sometimes, their impending death. When one gets so accustomed to witnessing death firsthand, merely breathing can constitute staying **alive**.

From birth I have been vibrantly **alive**. I am the youngest of five children and have always had a love for the stage as I continuously enjoyed the smiles my performing put on other people's faces. It brought joy to my heart. As I grew up and became keenly interested and amazed by the human body, I wanted to combine that with my love for people. Becoming a nurse seemed like a perfect fit, so I became one. I wanted to help people experience health to its fullest and give them the gift of feeling truly "**alive**".

After years of bedside nursing, I realized I was not in the health care profession at all. I was in sick care. I was watching people lose their only true asset in life, their health. They could not buy it back. It didn't care who their daddy was or how much money they had in the bank. I asked myself, "Why do we wait until sickness takes hold, and our health is gone, before we really value our health at all? What are we doing to contribute to the madness? Is it stoppable?" Several of my nurse friends got diagnosed with cancer in a short period of time and I sarcastically wondered if the sickness was caused by the hospital building itself. My mind and heart began to awaken.

Later that year I received a call from my sister. She wanted me to try some products she was using. She was experiencing great results from them. She decided she wanted to have her own business with this company so she could put her children first. She was a single mom with three girls. The youngest, Delaney, had cystic fibrosis. My sister wanted to be home with them every day, as she had been before her recent divorce. She had to be available for Delaney whenever she fell ill. I wanted that for her as well. I especially wanted that for my niece, Delaney. However, my sister was talking crazy. She was telling me she was going to earn a white Mercedes Benz and live her dreams. I was skeptical, to say the least, but supportive. Although I wanted no part of a business "like that," I was 100% on board to help her. I love my sister deeply and I wanted to help her in any way I could. I asked my friends to try some products and they were blown away with the quality of them and the results they experienced. Suddenly, I had a friend who wanted to join her in the business, so I agreed to look at it, too. Having no intention of making this my life's passion, I still decided to accompany my sister to the company's national convention in our hometown of St. Louis, Missouri. After all, it was going to provide us sister-time with no children and since I had four little ones, I was in! We met there and I was totally unprepared for the shift my life was about to take.

It is there that I would meet Rita Davenport for the first time. There were 17,000 attendees but I was sure Rita was talking directly to me as she spoke. I felt like I was the only one in the arena. I had never experienced the type of love that exuded from Rita as she spoke to the crowd that day. Through laughter and tears, I heard her painting a beautiful vision of becoming a people builder, building a tremendous life for my family, while loving other people enough to help them build the life they dreamt of for theirs. She spoke of being more and loving more, so you can give back to the world in a greater way. She shook my world with her message of hope and love. She expanded the vision I now have for helping more people to experience a better life. This new vision became so much greater than I had imagined when I first agreed to help my sister. She opened my mind to the limitless possibilities for those who felt they had no opportunity. She taught me that I could have more than I ever imagined by helping others get what they wanted most. Attaining all I desire in life by helping others have what they truly desire seemed to be an incredible way to succeed and to live.

I began to feel alive. My desire to help people was real and significant and so many people need this message of hope. Owning and designing my own life was actually possible and I wanted just that. I wanted to put God first, my family second, and my career third. And I would do all of this while impacting people and helping them become the best versions of themselves! I would be fully **alive**, taking care of myself, my health and teaching others to do the same. Rita spoke of earning that Mercedes Benz, just as my sister had mentioned. I realized it was not a figment of her imagination. It was not only real, but actually attainable. This was a legitimate business model, a reputable company that contained a caliber of women I had never seen before. People building people and doing amazing things with their financial freedom across the world. I was scared out of my mind, but decided to jump in with both feet anyway.

I returned to Florida and gathered my closest friends. I showed them the business plan and asked them if anyone else had ever offered them anything better? Three of my best friends said yes and together, we were unstoppable. I was picking out and driving a beautiful white Mercedes Benz just three short months later. I was on top of the world. I was both humbled and amazed. I learned to set goals and reached them. I learned the pains of leadership as well as the incredible rewards. I wanted so badly for everyone to experience this same success. Finally, I felt fully "**alive!**" I WAS fully "**alive!**" I was living a dream come true!

For the next several years I was making more money than I ever had in nursing. I was working part time and driving a beautiful car paid for by my company. I was sharing the vision and living the dream. My children were experiencing all-expense-paid five star vacations and they learned how to dream themselves. I was growing into the person I know I was born to become. This uncovered my passions. I realized there was so much more I wanted to accomplish.

In 2011, I received a call that my sister was sending her daughters to live with me and she would follow once loose ends were tied. I was elated to finally have the opportunity to live by family and experience the joys of having family close. The girls moved in and I was instantly the caregiver and second mom to Delaney, my sister's youngest daughter. Delaney was like no other child her age, she had a unique innocence and pureness of heart, she was the closest thing to an angel I have ever known. She was sweet, beautiful and her smile had everlasting impact. Unbeknownst to her, she became our greatest teacher. She taught us to love the unlovely, to ask important questions, never to worry. She taught us how to choose to see the best in everyone and most importantly, not to take anything too seriously. These are just a few of her life's lessons. We laughed and we loved in a whole new way, as she became one of us. She, in essence, completed our family.

It was May 2012 and Delaney was hospitalized for her regular cystic fibrosis tune-up. We were dancing and singing in her room, making the most of the inconvenience and pain of this disease. She was the life and light of the unit. She got her usual antibiotics and she was home again with IV antibiotics to complete the therapy. She was in and out of the hospital for the next five months. Something felt different with each hospitalization. She never seemed to go back to her baseline "normal." Her mother and I were continually reassured that everything was "fine" and Delaney was too healthy to be considered for a double-lung transplant, yet our instincts were telling us otherwise. She fell ill over Thanksgiving weekend and returned to the hospital for another lengthy stay. She managed to make it home for Christmas, just to return again on January 2, 2013. She was vibrant one moment and lifeless the next. I was keenly aware that breathing was not living. I watched her struggle to get each and every breath. My beautiful niece was eventually placed on life support to give her lungs a break and allow her to "rest." Realizing we were in a fight for Delaney's life, I laid down all my responsibilities at home and in my Arbonne business to be 100% present and available for my sister and 'our girl'.

I knew deep within I was called to walk this journey with my sister, as this is a path no human can nor should ever walk alone. Despite the exhaustion from living in an ICU and getting little to no sleep day after day, I was totally fully **alive**, using every ounce of strength to believe for her complete healing. I believed if I was not fully **alive**, there would be no hope for her to be. There would be four more months, three different pediatric intensive care units in three different hospitals, along with countless moments of fear, pain, anxiety and intense sadness. Mixed in, was the inability for me to catch my own breath at the realization of what was actually happening. Delaney now had become too sick to be considered for the double-lung transplant. We would have the privilege of experiencing her smile and communicating with her only a handful of times before she would make her journey into heaven on March 12, 2013 at the tender age of 15. Although we witnessed many miracles throughout our journey and experienced God's presence, grace and love in unbelievable ways, this was our final miracle. She was now fully **alive** in the presence of angels. Her body was no longer broken. However, we were dead. There wasn't anything left in me. I began to feel pain and darkness in the deepest way imaginable. In addition to my own pain, I was experiencing the pain of my whole family, pain that felt unbearable.

Today I know what it means to go through the motions of life. I know what it means to feel dead inside. I know that I DON'T WANT TO SIMPLY EXIST! I want to feel **alive** again as she is **alive**. Not only do I want to be **alive**, but I want to have new conversations with people about what it means to them to be **alive**. I want people to be awakened to what is going on in their bodies before it is too late. I want to teach them how to live fully **alive**, to really feel it every day.

Although Delaney had no responsibility in her illness, it was a genetic inheritance (neither of her parents were aware they carried this faulty gene), this is not the case for the majority of people. The vast population suffers and succumbs to chronic illnesses that are birthed from their very own lifestyle choices. Unfortunately, few people desire to converse about such topics before they are in a full-blown health crisis of their own. They refuse to see the value of the topic until their lives are directly affected by the cost or the inconvenience that sickness brings. It appears to be so much easier to have an invincible attitude and refuse to believe that such ailments could or would ever happen to them. If and when a diagnosis comes, it is so much easier to blame genetics and family history than to seek out root cause. As a matter of fact we have definitely decided to overlook root cause as an entire society. Our physicians are so quick to treat the screaming symptoms, rather than the underlying problems. As a result, we have been accustomed to a "quick" fix for our nagging ailments rather than take on the work of a real solution.

Disease is no respecter of persons; it finds its way into any human body that has weakened its ability to fight it off. The body is an amazing compensator, it will compensate on your behalf for years and years before it presents a cluster of symptoms we eventually label with the name of a disease. No other machine would be so kind for so long. If you or I treated our cars the way we do our bodies, we would find ourselves in for a very expensive repair much sooner, or we would be forced to find alternative transportation. The human body has the most incredible system of compensation but it, too, will eventually fail. What would happen if you put the incorrect fuel into your car? Let's say you have decided that unleaded gasoline is just way too expensive to use, so you hooked your car up to your garden hose and filled it up. The gas gage would peg the "F" meaning full, but how long do you think the car would run? Certainly not years, not even minutes. You would not only do serious damage to your engine, but you would be unable to make it to your final destination. This would be extremely inconvenient and expensive.

In essence we do this to our bodies every single day. We are tired, hungry and in need of fuel. So we find the easiest, often the cheapest, fuel put it in our bodies and expect to run on the highway of our lives at full speed. Since the body compensates so well, we are, in fact, able to do just that for many years. Eventually, the first warning lights begin to flash. We are tired, heavier than we have ever been, having headaches, body aches, as we begin to "feel our age". Chronic disease is born years before we have any true knowledge of it. There is a slow chipping away of our health on the cellular level until the clusters of symptoms are labeled a disease. Then in an effort to save ourselves, and return to "our highway of life" at full speed, we seek a quick fix, an easy way out. With no time for the inconvenience these speed bumps bring, we run to our physician and seek a magic pill only to find ourselves a year or two later with a bag full of medications, many of which we are unsure why we are taking. Our doctors are treating "risk factors" for diseases by prescribing medications that must be continued for a lifetime in order to lower things like blood pressure, blood sugar and cholesterol. These are symptoms of diseases not underlying causes. Why is the blood pressure elevated in the first place? We have now entered the "sick care" system and are on a slippery slope to death. The top diseases of our country are not only preventable but they are treatable, and even reversible, when we learn to find and to treat the underlying cause.

The conversations I have with people now are centered around being **alive** and **stay-n-alive** in order to live their calling, to fulfill their life's passion and mission. So I ask you... How are you stay-n-alive? Do you realize every choice you make each day leads you down the path of wellness or the pathway to disease? The small daily steps you choose down the road of wellness can give you huge results in providing you the ability to avoid pain and experience the beauty and joy of great long-term health.

It is time for you to embrace the healthiest version of yourself, to fuel your life with the vibrant energy it takes to remain truly **alive**. Knowing that you are feeling **alive** every step of your journey, allowing you to reach your own unique destination.

About the Author

Sharise Deimeke is an RN, turned "mompreneuer," who specializes in life-style medicine. She enjoys speaking to groups of people who are seeking ways to improve their energy, while protecting their long- term health. She partners with individuals who wish to decrease medication intake, and have an increased vitality and sense of wellbeing using a more holistic approach. Sharise designs strategies allowing people to increase their daily productivity, helping them to lose unwanted inches and pounds, but most importantly, keeping their cells in optimal health to prevent chronic diseases. Her message is affecting generational change.

Sharise has a passion for mentoring people who wish to help themselves and others have an incredible stream of residual income by redirecting their current spending while increasing their own health and wellness.

Sharise resides in Florida with her "rocket scientist" husband, three daughters and one son.

Visit her at www.sharisedeimeke.com

Like me on Facebook: Stay-n-alive

Twitter: @ShariseDeimeke

Out of the Blue

Rita Davenport

An excerpt from...
"Funny Side Up... A Southern Girl's Guide to Love, Laughter and Money"

I read in the paper a story about a woman and her five children who had been turned away from a shelter for battered women and children. As much as they wanted to take her in, they were jammed to the gunnels and just couldn't take another body into their building. In fact, they were in the middle of urgently seeking more funds so they could enlarge their facility. Their office was only a double wide trailer.

The woman turned around and went back home. When her husband found out where she had gone to try to get help, he grabbed a pair of scissors and stabbed her to death, right in front of their children.

When I heard this, it made me absolutely heartsick. The idea that there was this wonderful place staffed by people who were qualified to help and desperately wanted to help but who couldn't, simply because they didn't have the physical space...this was something I just could not abide. But what could I do? I didn't have the extra cash to give them myself, and with my plate so ridiculously full I didn't' see how I could possibly put in the time to organize and spearhead a major fund-raising effort.

Maybe you've heard that we often get our best ideas when we're in an environment with lots of negative ions, like out in the country, at a mountain late or by the seashore. For me, it's generally when I'm shaving my legs in the bathtub. I'm guessing God figures this is the only time I'm sitting still in one place long enough to listen.

So, I was in the aforementioned sanctified place one night, shaving away, and the thought came into my head: *You have to raise $150,000 for the Sojourner Center.* No burning bush, no voice of thunder and no wondrous signs. Just me, my Lady Remington, and the impossible thought plunked right down in the middle of my head.

Oh, Lord, I thought. How on earth am I going to do that - you know how busy I am!

Then I got to thinking. I'd helped a lot of people over the years, sometimes just by virtue of having them as a guest on the show. I was the hostess and producer of an award winning local talk show for 15 years. I was considered the "Skinny White Poor Oprah of Arizona". The show had various segments, similar to today's morning shows. We covered news, weather, television & movies, philanthropy, crafts and cooking. The show went from *Phoenix at Midday* to *Open House* and then to *Cooking with Rita*. Over the time I hosted the show, I was privileged to have interviewed many Hollywood celebrities, sports celebrities, authors, speakers and local proprietors. For example, there was a retired firefighter who had invested everything he had into creating a little paint store that had not done well and was on the verge of closure. I heard about his situation and invited him onto the show to demonstrate faux painting. He told us that the day before he was on the show; he had sold a total of one paintbrush. When he opened up the morning after our show, there was a line of customers waiting, and he was able to keep his doors open after all.

I decided to squeeze a little time out of my days to start calling people, and keep calling until I'd found 150 people who would each contribute $1,000. That shouldn't take long, right?

Ha. I pretty quickly found out how well *that* idea worked. Soon it felt like it would be easier to get 1,500 people to give me $100 each...or maybe get 150,000 to each give me a dollar. Days went by and I wasn't getting anywhere. I didn't see how on earth I was ever going to get that $150,000 together - but I *had* to.

And then, out of the blue, the man who had owned the failing paint store called.

"I heard you were raising money for the Sojourner Center," he said. I have no idea how he'd heard this. He was not on the list of those I'd called; that list had been limited to people whom I knew were quite well off. But here he was, on my phone. "Rita," he said," I don't think I've ever thanked you enough for having me on your show. You may not realize just what an impact that one day had."

No, I admitted, I really didn't. I knew he had been able to keep his store open, and I was thrilled about that. But that's as far as I knew the story.

"Well let me tell you the rest," he said. "Today my little paint store is worth eight million dollars. I am a wealthy man because you invited me to be on your show and you showcased my business. I want you to know I'm putting a check in the mail to you today, for Sojourner Center, and I hope you'll accept it."

He sent me a check for $15,000, and when word got around it got the ball rolling. My dear assistant, Tami Taase set up a chart in our office that looked like a giant thermometer to measure donations, with a goal at the top of $150,000. Before long, I had the full amount I was called to raise.

Since then, from fundraisers, family, friends and colleagues, our donations have grown to over two million dollars. Sojourner now offers shelter to hundreds of domestic violence victims and their children on two campuses in Arizona. The need is still great, though, since domestic violence is an epidemic affecting over 25 percent of our population. You can find their website at www.sojournercenter.org.

When you do for others, you *will* get a return. You won't necessarily know where it's going to come from or how - but I promise you, it *will* come.

The following are a few *"Ritaisms"*. They are one-liners, memorable things that her followers have heard Rita say over the years that have had an impact on their lives. Some are profound, some are funny, some are just plain silly... and ALL are 100 percent Rita!

- We need to love ourselves before we love others.
- God didn't make any junk.
- Don't hang around with people who are more messed up than you are.
- Don't let people *should* on you. Often people tell us what we *should* or *shouldn't* do. In fact, sometimes, you *should* on yourself.
- From now on don't *should* on yourself.
- Keep calm and carry on.

- Put your big girl panties on and deal with it!
- Money isn't everything, but its right up there with oxygen.
- When someone says *no*, that just means they don't *know* enough yet.
- You have to circulate to percolate.
- Get your *ask* in gear!
- Be more, have more, learn more, and earn more so you can share more.
- Take your business seriously, but don't take yourself too seriously.
- There is nothing sexier than a rich woman and I remind my husband of that frequently.
- Do a little more than is expected of you.
- A hand out is not as good as a hand up.
- If money will fix it, it's not a problem.
- Rewards are in proportion to your service.
- Love what is.

About the Author

Rita Davenport is an internationally recognized expert in the principles of success, time management, goal setting, creative thinking, and self esteem and confidence. Her unique background as an entrepreneur, corporate executive, author, speaker, humorist, and broadcaster sets her apart and has made her one of the most beloved and widely admired role models on the speaking circuit.

She produced and hosted her own award winning television shows in Phoenix, Arizona for 15 years, and has been inducted into the Arizona Broadcasters Association's Hall of Fame. Rita has appeared as a guest on more than 200 radio and television shows.

As a speaker, Rita has been called motivational, challenging, humorous, personal and powerful. As a charter member of the National Speakers Association and NSA Hall of Famer, she has shared the platform with such notables as Erma Bombeck, Les Brown, Jack Canfield, Dr. Wayne Dyer,

Mark Victor Hansen, Tom Hopkins, John Maxwell, Og Mandino, Denis Waitley and Zig Ziglar.

Rita has written three books that have sold over one million copies, including the best seller, *Making Time, Making Money* and two cookbooks, *Sourdough Cookery* and *DeGrazia & Mexican Cookery*, with famed Southwestern artist Ted DeGrazia.

Rita feels that her most outstanding accomplishments have been as wife to her high school sweetheart, David, and mother to her two sons, Michael and Scott, and Nana to her grandchildren. She resides in Scottsdale, Arizona, with her husband.

Connect with Rita at http://ritadavenport.com/ and www.facebook.com/OfficialRitaDavenport

Living the Dream

Robin Wong

The sun was beaming across the sky, warm ocean waves crashed against the shore, the joyous sounds of laughter dancing in our ears, surrounding us at every point in our journey. Only 2 months earlier, this quiet community was like a scary little ghost town. There was no laughter. Everyone was sad. Kids sat quietly alone in the streets with nowhere to go and nothing to do.

I was so excited to be on this two month trip of a lifetime! Three of my friends and I were on this journey with a massive goal of transforming lives. I was in the middle of living my dream! This trip had been in my heart for many years and now it was a reality. Even my goose bumps were excited!

I remember the day we were escorted into town and given the "low down" on what was happening and what these amazing people needed to survive. They had no clean water, no school and, according to them, "they had no life." We knew this was going to be the greatest experience of our lives, and since we had much work to do and were seeing some horrible things, it was also going to be the biggest challenge of our lives. We had learned so much about the organizations around the world that were making a difference and knew deep down in our hearts that we could make a difference too! Our lives would never be the same after this journey!

As the work began, there was a continual flow of love; it was intense and it was beautiful. Slowly, but surely, the people realized what was happening and their hearts were blossoming to this strange and wonderful new experience. It was amazing to watch the people as they embraced the work that had to be done. The smiles on their faces, as I remember them now, are indescribable, and the picture that remains in my mind is priceless.

We had our first day off from 3 weeks of working with the locals to plan, build and implement a school. With each passing day, we could see more and more kids smiling, chatting and bringing the gift of laughter and dance to the streets. It was awesome! The people grew in numbers as they watched, smiled, laughed and participated with us as the school we were building started to take shape. One kid followed me around everywhere. He was so cool, so my friend Teresa and I named him "Mr. Breeze" as he was there by our sides for the entire experience pouring water on us to keep us cool.

This experience went on for two months, we had new friendships, we feasted together, we danced and even my lame jokes got a few laughs. At the end of each very long and rewarding day, the 4 of us sat near the baby blue ocean watching the sun wave goodbye to us, always with a slightly different smile. As the time flew by way too fast, we could only look at each other with admiration for a job well done and for sharing this amazing adventure together.

It was our last Sunday when all the children came around to give us a token of appreciation for what we had done. They made little heart bracelets with the word "love" on them. They also gave us teeny little rocks with their names painted on each one! "Wow" was our response, as tears once again came pouring down our faces like an endless stream of water for the 60th day in a row. Once again, we laughed, cried, hugged and vowed to return to this community! We had a day full of love and happiness, mixed with dancing, playing, singing and food! I was also the little drummer boy playing bongos although I've never done that before. They could tell.

In the afternoon, our wonderful guides, Mark and Sarah, surprised us with an excursion into the mountains for an experience of a lifetime in the jungle. We walked a few miles with most of the people from the community tagging along in anticipation of another amazing day! We had the opportunity to ride wild horses through the forest, and walk on a crazy scary flimsy ladder across the jungle river. The funniest part, at least to them, was when I fell in the water while showing off. There was laughter everywhere, as I frantically scrambled out of the water being chased by Thor, the local alligator!

At the end of the day, the entire community shocked and surprised us once again by presenting us cry babies with Humanitarian awards that made us weep just a little bit more! I knew right then and there that doing this kind of work and being on this beautiful path was right, and that I would spend the rest of my days leading, teaching and inspiring others to do the same.

On the way to the airport, tears still in our eyes, we reminisced about the trip and how we were able to make a huge difference. We thought about our other adventures, but this challenge was by far the most incredible and rewarding experience of our lives!

When we arrived home, we were so tired, but still flying high. While driving, I got a very exciting and surprising text from my favorite actress, Meg Ryan. She and some of her friends heard about the mission and our Humanitarian Award and wanted to come along on the next trip. Since I've been in love with her since I was 2, I said Yes!!

And then it happened! Aaaaaaah ...I WOKE UP!!

I don't know if you've ever had a dream like this, but this is one I never wanted to wake up from. We have the ability to dream, to visualize, to manifest, to join forces with others and do anything our hearts desire! That's what I want you to understand, and perhaps my story will put you in the frame of mind needed to make a real difference in your life and in this world!

Did any of this stuff happen? Nope, not exactly like that but, Wow, did it ever plant a seed in my heart that life can be a lot different if we just look at things in a more positive light.

It's amazing how telling you that story fires me up even more to do exactly what was described, except for the Alligator part; I don't ever want to experience that again!

In our dreams and visualizations is where we often feel the most alive, so maybe our dreams are guides to where we should go and what we should do. I remember waking up many times trying desperately to bring the dream back, feeling frustrated because it was over. After awhile though, you start thinking and feeling differently about what you can do and you start desiring to make things happen.

I remember always saying to myself, "This is an awesome dream but I want to go back to sleep and stay asleep as long as I can." My thoughts are different now, because when I dream like this, I say, "I want to wake up and do this as fast as I can." Wow, what a difference and what a beautiful way to think!

I want you to know that it's ok to dream, and I'm not just talking about closing your eyes, falling asleep and hoping that some good things show up that night. I'm talking about closing your eyes, visualizing your passions and desires, thinking positive thoughts and seeing a manifestation of your dreams.

Think about this for a minute! Have your dreams become your reality? Will you stop at nothing to make sure you live the life you desire? Will you do whatever it takes to make a difference in your life and in the lives of those you care about? There are so many questions we could ask ourselves, but the key is to go deep inside to discover what really turns you on! For me, everything in that dream turns me on and I believe that when we impact the lives of others, we make a massive impact on our own life! Is that something you want to do?

For the longest time, I didn't believe I could change the world, didn't believe I could make a difference, and I couldn't even imagine being able to change someone else's life! Like most people, I was having enough of a challenge changing my own. The beautiful thing about visualization and dreaming is that in your dreams, everything is possible! We can participate in our dreams and we have the ability to create, out of nothing, something magnificent. Do you believe that? If you do, that's a great starting point for a wonderful life! When you are dreaming, there are no self imposed limitations! Maybe it's time to dream again!

This is kind of funny, but in school, I used to get in trouble for daydreaming all the time. I find it hilarious and ironic that I now encourage and teach people how to do it! And remember, kids, not in school though, okay?

"The two most important days in your life are the day you are born and the day you find out why."
~ Mark Twain

Sometimes what keeps us back from acting on our dreams is we haven't decided or discovered who we are. When you discover who you are and why you are here, magic starts to happen - you just have to believe in yourself!

I've learned so much. It's also taken me quite some time to understand that everything, even our failures and frustrations, are valuable learning experiences. I've also learned that I have the power to turn my dreams into my reality!

Some Significant Steps to
Turn Your Dreams into Reality

Make a Committed Decision

When you believe in something, and you have a burning desire to make it happen, the first step involves making a decision, and not just a decision, but a committed one!

"The secret to happiness is to be happy."
~ Dalai Lama

I remember when I met the Dalai Lama and he said that. Well, he's right, happiness is a choice; it is a positive decision that can change your life when you are committed to being happy. There are so many different decisions you can make, why not choose the one that makes you feel great!

"It's in your moments of decision that your destiny is shaped." ~ Anthony Robbins

Decide for yourself what is possible and then just go out and make it happen!

When you make a decision that is meaningful to you, it is important to Act on it right away. For example, when I launched into the reality of my dream to make a difference and change the world, my first action was to start connecting with like-minded partners, finding time to brainstorm, plan and implement my passions and desires. Remember, you can do it, just make the committed decision to get started.

Create your own Culture

This is simply creating the environment that allows your Best to be present at all times. That has been a struggle for me, and I also know that in your greatest struggle comes your ultimate success. It involves figuring out all the things that will help make your life run smoother, so that you can have the ability to dream and move forward in a positive direction. Let me share a few thoughts on what I believe can assist you in achieving your own culture.

There is an obvious transition time between a dream and the reality of it! There is always an in-between-time where thoughts and experiences of the past are still there. Lingering in our lives and in our thoughts are consequences of past decisions, and limiting beliefs that can be a challenge to move past. You can move forward! One thing to remember is to have a short term memory of your mistakes. We all make mistakes, so instead of tripping over the stepping stones of life, embrace them. I invite you to gently walk over them, recognizing that they are a learning experience on the pathway of growth. Why not fail forward a little faster! Move on from your mistakes, chalk them up to another learning experience and keep growing. Babies are a perfect example of this; just watch them trying to walk, falling over and over again, and never quitting. Although this sounds odd, we have to learn to fail quickly because that allows us to learn how to grow even more quickly.

Our other choice would be to just stand there doing nothing and hoping we can figure it all out without falling. This, as you can imagine simply doesn't work, so don't fear falling down. It's simply the process of growing and expanding you into the person big enough to accomplish the dream. Once you create this type of "culture attitude," like a rocket, you're ready to launch!

To continue creating your own culture, surround yourself with positive, like minded people who are optimistic, are moving forward and who also want to make a difference in this world. This book is filled with stories by authors who are making a difference in the world in one way or another. Each one of them has "created their own culture" and I encourage you to connect in conversation with us anytime, so we can be part of your own new culture.

Create a focused effort

Reaching your dreams and creating your life takes a focused effort. We must recognize this and take action toward our results. There are two kinds of dreamers, those who *wish* and those who *will*. You cannot wish your way to achieving your unique greatness and fulfilling your dreams although that's a great start. You take a step of effort in the direction of your dreams, then another, then another. And when things get difficult, you WILL yourself to take even another. Along the way, you will discover that not only does each step bring you closer to your dreams; it also grows you into a stronger and more vibrant person. Most people don't take the first step because they immediately say they can't do it. The situation, the passion or the dream may look too big or too difficult, and if you never take the first step, you will never get started!

This focused effort is so exhilarating and energizing when applied to what makes you come alive. In other words, if whatever your dreams are resonates with who you are, and you develop a burning desire in your heart to make it happen, you will not only have the energy required to make it a reality, you will also thoroughly enjoy the amazing journey to its accomplishment.

What makes YOU come alive? Make the effort to live it, love it and share it!

When we live our passions, we inspire others to live theirs. My dream is that you will be inspired by what I have shared and that you will use these lessons to make your life the best it can be. Whatever your passions and desires are, start believing in them. Believe in yourself! Make a committed decision to get started, create the culture you desire, and put forth a focused effort to make your dreams become your reality. When you combine these three significant steps, great things will always happen! I encourage you now to dream, visualize, get around others, be around me, stay in touch with my awesome fellow authors, and make the Rest of your Life the Best of your Life!

It's never too late to "Live your Dream!"

About the Author

Robin Wong is also known as Mr. Karma Junkie. As the name implies, he "gets high" from helping others. Making a Difference and Changing the World is Robin's heartfelt passion and his purpose. Aligning himself with others who love to inspire, Robin is dedicated to the success of others. He lives by the promise to serve all the people he meets with honesty, integrity and love.

Robin is now living his own dream as one of the creators of the Global Optimist, a community with a global vision "*To move the world forward through the 'Power of Best'.*"

Learn more about Robin at: http://mrkarmajunkie.com/

And learn more about the "Global Optimist" by visiting: http://globaloptimist.com

Connect with him at robin@globaloptimist.com

Why Not?

Sharon Lechter

We have all heard about "finding your 'why,'" and how important it is for reaching true success and happiness. But what happens when you can't figure out your "why?" Maybe it's time to try a few "why not's?"

In 1979, I was 25 living in Atlanta and miserable… even though I was a rising star in a Big Eight Accounting Firm. I was working all the time, had no social life and I kept thinking that if I was going to be working that hard, it should be for myself instead of everyone else. I had grown up in an entrepreneurial home and seen my parents build businesses and invest in real estate. But my course had been different. My parents dream was that I would get a college degree and great job with a company with a great pension…and things were going well for me according to that plan…except I was miserable.

My own entrepreneurial spirit hit me over the head one night. A client called me on the phone and offered me an ownership position in a company in which he was investing in New Hampshire. It had an innovative new technology and I had the opportunity to get in on the ground floor. How exciting! So I remember sitting on my bed with a tablet writing the pros and cons of changing professions.

Did it have a large upside? Yes… a pro.

Could I always come back to public accounting? Yes… another pro.

Would leaving interfere with the fast track I was on, if I wanted to come back? Probably...definitely a con.

Was there a risk? Yes...another con.

Did I really want to move so far north where I didn't know anyone? Yet... another con.

This was as far as I got and suddenly my hand took over and wrote across the top of the page "WHY NOT?"

I stared at the page for the longest time...and realized I couldn't answer that question. Instead of being a conservative accountant wanting all the answers to the question, "WHY?" I decided to take a leap of faith and say, "Why Not?" I made the decision **at that moment** to accept my client's (soon to be partner's) offer... and I was off to New Hampshire. But that was only the beginning of the story.

So how did it work out? Not exactly according to any plan I had written or imagined. Within just a couple of months I had uncovered an absolute mess...financials that were filled with errors and omissions, a computer system in shambles, and risky decisions that had been made by the prior executive team that I felt were definitely in the "grey" zone. I was terrified and feared that if I stayed I might be risking my professional credentials as a CPA. What a colossal mistake I had made. I took a couple of weeks off to contemplate what my next career move would be. My self-esteem had disappeared...going from being on the top of the world just months earlier to hiding from it.

The day I returned to the company I found lawyers at our offices, lawyers from the opposing side of a legal action that had been started well before I had joined the company. I had not been involved in the legal aspects of the case but knew it had to do with some on-going patent litigation. They were performing "discovery" which means they were looking through our documents to find evidence to support their claims in the case. The lawyers had been kind enough to wait for me to return to go through my office and apparently had "elected" one attorney to search my office. His name was Michael Lechter.

Yes, I met my future husband when he was "going through my drawers!"...literally! He was sitting in my desk chair when I came in and we shook hands over my desk...and there was an electric shock that we both felt. It truly was "Love at first sight!"

Thankfully, the love at first sight reaction was a mutual experience and Michael asked me to move to Maryland where he lived. So now I knew where I was going...but still didn't know what I would be doing. Michael and I were married nine months later and just celebrated 34 years together.

The moment I met Michael was the answer to my question, "what and where for the next chapter in my life?" But it had all started when I asked myself that night in Atlanta sitting on my bed, 'Why not?" and then acted on it.

At that moment, I had decided to conquer the fear of the unknown...instead of asking "Why?" I chose to ask myself, "Why Not?" It has become the guiding principle in my life ever since.

The actual decision to go with the company was a colossal mistake from a business point of view, but it was the absolute right decision for the rest of my life. As Napoleon Hill said, "Every adversity, every failure, every heartache carries with it the seed on an equal or greater benefit."

I have made plenty of mistakes in my life, and had several such major events that have defined the person I have become. My oldest son went off to college in 1992 and got himself into credit card debt within the first few months. I was so angry at him, but even more so at myself. I thought I had taught him about money...I had taught him the lessons my parents had taught me. But there had not been credit cards when I went to college and while my son had been with me when I used my credit cards, he was not with me when I paid them off each month. My husband and I refused to bail him out and it took him seven years to get out of debt and repair his credit rating. My son's credit card debacle turned out to be another major event in my life.

That experience with my son and my anger over the lack of financial education in schools ignited a new passion and I dedicated the rest of my professional career to creating financial education tools and teaching the importance of taking control of your financial life. This may not have happened had my son not gotten into so much debt. Again I asked myself, "Why Not?" Why not do something about what made me so mad? So instead of being embarrassed about my son's experience, I used it as a catalyst to define the direction of my career.

And as they say... the rest is history. A few years later I co-authored *Rich Dad Poor Dad* and 14 other books in the Rich Dad series and built the Rich Dad Company to become an international voice in financial empowerment. In 2001, my husband and I were in Beijing, China for a speaking tour I was doing to promote the books and we were visiting a local mall when a dozen young girls in school uniforms ran up to us asking if they could practice their English on us. We said yes, of course, and they started talking about a book they were studying in school that they loved and how it had opened their eyes to the world of business, *Rich Dad Poor*

Dad. At that moment I was frozen with a combination of disbelief and joy, while my husband smiled and asked them if they had the book with them. As one girl eagerly handed him her copy he pointed to my picture on the back of the book and then to me. They all started screaming and jumping up and down...and of course dozens of pictures followed. That night I was still in awe realizing that something that started from my anger at the lack of financial education, and asking myself "'why not' do something about it?" could have resulted in that kind of impact on the other side of the world in just a few years.

At that time I believed that building the Rich Dad brand was my life's work and my most important accomplishment. But it turned out that building the Rich Dad Organization was merely a stepping stone... there was much more for me to do.

In 2007 and at the height of our success at the Rich Dad Company I found myself miserable once again. My personal mission was no longer aligned with my partners' in the Rich Dad organization and I made the decision to leave this very successful company. I am sure you have heard the expression, "When one door closes, another opens." My life has certainly been a living example of that phrase.

Little did I know that within just a few months of making the decision to leave the Rich Dad Organization, several events would occur that made me realize that my career in financial education had truly just begun.

First, I formed my own company *Pay Your Family First* and began creating experiential and affordable products originally aimed for young adults...coming full circle to where my true passion had started with my son's trouble years earlier. In creating these products like *ThriveTime for*

Teens it felt like a direct download from my own life of experience...and it was a great relief!

Then, just a few months later I received a call from the White House inviting me to join the first President's Advisory Council on Financial Literacy. I had the honor of serving our President...but more importantly it gave me a national voice that allowed me to highlight the importance of financial and entrepreneurship education. In 2009 the Credit Card Accountability Responsibility and Disclosure Act was passed that no longer allowed credit card companies to solicit students on campus. While I certainly cannot take credit for the Act, I was definitely one of the squeaky wheels asking for it.

And then another call came in...and it was from the CEO of the Napoleon Hill Foundation. My husband and I had known Don Green for several years and had great respect for his leadership in keeping the works and wisdom of Napoleon Hill alive around the world. I had first read Hill's most famous work, *Think and Grow Rich,* when I was 19 years old and didn't realize the impact it had on me...until that call. It was March 20, 2008, when Don Green called and asked me to step into a project called *Three Feet From Gold.* I was speechless, but quickly responded with, "Absolutely!" It felt like I had been invited home because my passion and mission were so aligned with those of the Foundation. Have you ever had the feeling that the stars were aligned in your own life? I did at that moment.

Greg Reid and I went on to co-author *Three Feet From Gold* which highlights Hill's philosophy of perseverance and "never giving up." We interviewed 35 of today's successful leaders about not just their success stories, but how they made it through the darkest times and persevered to build their great successes. It reveals the power of association and became a national bestseller. The month we released the book in 2009, I had two additional calls that became new "major events" for me, one from the American Society of Certified Public Accountants and another call from Don Green.

It seemed my professional life had come full circle in the twilight of my career, as the AICPA asked me to join their National CPAs Financial Literacy Commission to serve as a national spokesperson to promote financial literacy. It was an incredible honor to serve as a spokesperson and they also asked me to serve as the editor of the AICPA's first mass market book on financial education, *Save Wisely Spend Happily,* released in October 2012. In December 2013, they acknowledged me as an AICPA Financial Literacy Champion. And it all started from my concerns as a parent!

Another call from Don Green in 2009 was equally life-changing. He asked me to review a newly discovered manuscript that Napoleon Hill had written in 1938, just after he published *Think and Grow Rich*, the bestselling personal development and business book of all time. He had titled the manuscript *Outwitting the Devil* and had intended it to be published as the sequel to *Think and Grow Rich.* However the manuscript scared Hill's wife and she forbid it from being published. It had been hidden for over 70 years. As I read it, it was as if Napoleon Hill was speaking directly to me. Even though it was written so long ago, it is a perfect message for people struggling during today's difficult economic times.

At the time he wrote it, Hill had become frustrated by the realization that even though people would read and learn the steps to becoming successful from *Think and Grow Rich,* many of them would still not reach the level of success they truly deserved. He wrote *Outwitting the Devil* in hopes that it would help people break through their fears and get past the self-limiting beliefs that were holding them back.

I believe the book being hidden for so many years was serving a higher and greater purpose. So many people today are paralyzed by fear, unable to deal with the economic troubles from the past few years. *Outwitting the Devil* may just be the right book at the right time. One reviewer wrote, *"Outwitting the Devil* will create a cosmic shift in positive outcomes."

In working on the book which was published in June of 2011, I truly felt at peace. The book helped me understand how fear had really held me back in my own life so many times, and yet it also showed me how I had been able to conquer that fear along the way. It brought true clarity behind my mantra of "Why Not?" When you live in fear, you live in a state of asking the question, "Why?" It gives you the excuse of not moving forward. It may prevent you from realizing your dreams. This fear is crippling and as Hill reveals, is the number one tool of a manmade devil.

Outwitting the Devil gave me the courage to once again "fight the system." I took my passion to the Arizona Legislature to try to change the educational system and I reached out to community leaders to join my call for change. As a result, SB 1449 was signed into law in June of 2013, creating a greater emphasis on the need for financial education proficiency as a graduation requirement. It is proof positive that one person with a mission fueled by passion and surrounded by the right team, truly can make positive change...and leave a legacy.

Have you asked yourself, "Why Not?" Are you charting a new course? Are you stepping outside the box, and revealing the unknown with eager anticipation of what the future may hold? You can challenge the status quo, and create the change you want to see!

Every decision you make, every phone call you receive, every trauma you experience creates an opportunity for a major event in your life. May you learn to recognize it, embrace it, step into the unknown and realize all that it has to offer to you. Instead of asking yourself, "Why?"...start asking yourself, "Why Not!"

May you be blessed with success!

About the Author

Sharon Lechter is an entrepreneur, author, philanthropist, educator, international speaker, licensed CPA and mother. She is the founder and CEO of Pay Your Family First, an organization dedicated to teaching the practical skills that will give a new generation the self-assurance to become masters, instead of slaves, to their money. Sharon is also the author of the bestselling books *Rich Dad Poor Dad, Outwitting the Devil, Three Feet From Gold* and her newest release, *Save Wisely, Spend Happily.* Sharon served as a member of the first President's Advisory Council on Financial Literacy, and is a national spokesperson for the AICPA's Commission on Financial Literacy. In 2013 Sharon received the designation of AICPA Financial Literacy Champion.

Sharon has recently been named the 2013 Woman of the Year by National Bank of Arizona and was honored by Az Business magazine as one of the 50 Most Influential Women in Arizona Business. She is a member on national boards of

Childhelp and Women Presidents' Organization; and international speaker and advocate for financial literacy.

Sharon's latest book, *Think and Grow Rich for Women* will be released on May 29,2014

Pre Order your copy at www.sharonlechter.com/women

The Law of Attraction in Action

Karen Mayfield's connection to Sharon Lechter.

In 1994, I created and was teaching a course on Peace of Mind. I was working with my own Peace of Mind Scale on a daily basis. In 2003, I purchased a copy of Napoleon Hill's *Grow Rich with Peace of Mind* at a garage sale for 25 cents. Reading this book expanded my understanding of peace of mind and changed my life. In fact, the Wake Up Women coaching program is a direct result of this book.

In Los Angeles in 2008, I was introduced to Greg Reid, who was co authoring *Think and Grow Rich--Three Feet From Gold* with Sharon Lechter. When I told Greg that I would like to do a project with the Napoleon Hill Foundation around the Peace of Mind course, he told me Sharon was the person I needed to talk with. As much as I intended to make that call to Sharon, life has its own way of happening. Shortly after that conversation with Greg, my husband died, and then my house got hit by a tornado. Calling Sharon was put on hold since other things had taken priority.

When Rita Davenport came on board as an author for this book, she said she would like Sharon Lechter to join us as well. Having Sharon as an author in this book is the Law of Attraction in action. I'm excited beyond words! Now I look forward to that conversation with Sharon about the Peace of Mind Course and the Napoleon Hill Foundation.

The Law of Attraction is always in action!

Letting Go of the HOW
Creates the Space for the WOW

Candi Parker

"Imagination is everything.
It is the preview of life's coming attractions."
~ Albert Einstein

Your imagination is your workshop where your dreams are fashioned. In your imagination, picture yourself as already having achieved your goals. See yourself doing the things that you'll be doing when you've reached your goals. When you visualize your goals and desires, you get your subconscious mind working toward making your mental pictures come true. The size of your goal does not matter.

This is true for anything you want to manifest. I had a long list and one of the things that I wanted was a brick patio that I had designed to be a part of the entrance to my house, which was under renovation. All of my funds had to go to the essentials and bricks were not on the list. Since visualizing works for me, I got right on it.

I staked out my patio area and when anyone came by I would point to the area and say, "This is where my patio made from old bricks is going to be" and I would go on to describe it and show them my unique design. I could see it in my mind's eye and I drew it to show others. I did not have the old bricks that I wanted to use for this patio, only the idea, so I just affirmed and believed that the patio would be made out of old used bricks and that I would eventually get them.

**Be alert always!
It creates inspired thought and ideas.**

I was always alert for old bricks. One day I was driving by the remains of an old house. The chimney was the only thing standing. I thought, "God, I sure would love to have those bricks for my patio." But, I couldn't just take them. So, I let go of the idea and drove on. A few days later, I happened to drive by the chimney again and had the same thought, "God, I sure would love to have those old bricks. They would be perfect for my patio." Well, I didn't know who owned them so, once again, I let go of the idea and kept on driving. I kept rationalizing and negating the possibility.

A week later I went by that place again and desired those bricks. Then...I noticed a truck at the empty restaurant building next door. Hmmm...maybe there was someone in there who I could have a conversation with that would know who owned the property and maybe they would let me have the bricks.

One of my favorite messages is:

When I have inspired thought, I act on it.

So, I turned around and circled back to the building. As I was walking towards the door, a woman was coming out of the building.

"Hi," I said to her, "is this your place?"

"Yes." She said, "Have you come for the bricks?"

54

What?!! My jaw dropped!

I told her that I did, but how did she know?

She said, "I've been praying someone would come and get those bricks because the city is going to clear the lot on Monday and I just knew someone could use them."

It was Saturday. I told her I would love to have the bricks and that I would be right back with some help. Off I went to get a rope and some help. In spite of comments to the contrary from the peanut gallery, I tied the rope around the chimney and to the back of my truck. I gently stepped on the gas and nothing happened! I stepped on the gas a little bit harder and again, nothing. I happened to look at the watchers and saw a smirk so... I gunned it (ha!) and I pulled that chimney down and it just fell apart because the mortar was dry and fragile. The bricks were separated from the mortar and just laid out for me. Because of this, I now have a beautiful patio made from old bricks in my entrance in a unique design I created.

I focused on the end result; an awesomely unique patio made from old bricks, and I did not get stuck in the "how", like looking for the money or figuring out how I was going to build it. I could not have planned or imagined how the bricks would show up and that they would come to me so easily and for free. All I had to do was know it and it would happen.

When we get attached to "how" we would like things to happen, we stop believing and dreaming. Forget the "how"; it happens by itself, you just have to know what you want and stay focused on it. Be a conscious chooser. Keep revising your list of what you desire to do, be and have. And know it is happening NOW!

You deserve all good. Keep yourself motivated. This is a new habit to cultivate. You are the only one who can do this for yourself. And you are the only one who can sabotage you. Find creative ways to get around judgmental thinking, yours included. You CAN do this, too; you just have to DO it.

"Whether you think you can or think you can't,
either way you are right." ~ Henry Ford

If you imagine all of the less than positive possibilities, then that is what will manifest. Focus on positive possibilities, keep thinking, dreaming and focusing on what you REALLY want to manifest and have in your life. Even the small stuff.

Just think, positive and negative thoughts cannot occupy your mind at the same time! If your mental chatter is less than positive, turn it around! What else can you focus on? Why - what you want, of course!

When you start to desire something in your life it is like you are planting a seed thought in your mind. When you negate the thought, well then, it's over. When you energize your seed thoughts, your choices, with positive visualization and actions, the seed takes hold and begins to grow and you are on your way to having what you want. When you don't pay attention to seed thoughts, your outcome is vastly different than when you nurture your seed thoughts with actions while believing in the positive outcome that you desire.

In nature, when you plant a seed, you grow a plant and then you harvest the results. When you don't care for your plant your harvest may not be what you may have anticipated. When you expect a harvest, you nurture the seeds with water and nutrients, and when they became seedlings, you continue to nurture them with water, weeding and feeding. Only then your expectations of a good harvest manifest with extraordinary results.

The nature of all energy works the same way. When you expect your desire to manifest and you nurture those thoughts, it has to come about.

What you think about, you bring about.
What you talk about, you create in your life.

Put yourself around people who believe in you. See yourself receiving your desires. What will that look like?

You may have been trained to pay attention to details and the "how" of doing things. This is new information and it may take some time to totally "get it." And just like anything, you get better at it with practice. Rather than worry about HOW something happens, focus on WHAT you want to see happen. This shifts your energy and your results.

The "how" is not your job!
Holding the vision of your desires is.

So, wherever you are right now, take a moment and "see" your dream in your mind's eye. Get to "know" it and believe!!!! When you believe it, you see it.

"When you believe it, when you can feel it, it will show up
for you. That is the Truth."
~Dr. Michael Bernard Beckwith

About the Author

Candi Parker is an Acupuncture Physician, author, certified Law of Attraction coach, book coach, book publisher and Army Veteran. Through personal experience and extensive research, she has created an effective system for tapping into the multi-billion dollar industry of eBook sales with her course, *Write a Kindle Book in a Weekend.* www.KindleBookInaWeekend.com

Her book, *Shift Happens: How I Won a Million Dollars with the Law of Attraction* is on Amazon in print and on Kindle.

The common theme in all Candi does is her passion and expertise in providing ways for people to achieve health, wealth and happiness.

Visit her websites: www.CandiParker.com
www.ParkerHouseBooks.com, and
www.PositiveTribe.com.

A Leap of Faith Becomes a Jump for Joy!

Judee Light

"Life is a daring adventure, or nothing." This is one of my favorite sayings and is attributed to Helen Keller, an amazing model of possibility on this planet. I like to see my life and my ever-evolving spiritual awareness journey as a daring adventure. I grow the most and feel most alive when I am facing my fears and expanding my comfort zone beyond its present limits.

Deliberately putting yourself outside your comfort zone is called adventure, and I have been a lover of adventure since I was a teenager. My inner spirit keeps "making me" have adventures!

Quite a number of years ago, I started keeping a list of adventures that I wanted to experience in this lifetime. Soon after I had written that list (when I was 48, divorced, recently self-employed and experiencing some financial challenges), I read in the local newspaper about a journalism student's experience of bungee jumping at the local fair. I enjoyed reading the article, yet didn't thing much more about it, as bungee jumping was certainly not on my list of adventures. I really didn't like heights . . . especially being at the top of them looking down.

The day after I read that article, I went camping with a friend overnight and we spent 24 hours in total silence with the intent of connecting with God (Creator, Source, Infinite Intelligence, whatever you want to call this Energy). I was inspired to do this short spiritual retreat after reading Jim Rosemergy's book, *Living the Mystical Life Today.* On the way home from that silent retreat, the bungee jump story suddenly popped into my thoughts. As soon as I got home, I got the article out and read it again. This time the story had a much greater impact on me. The reporter was telling about how he froze the first time the Jump Master said, "3, 2, 1 . . . bungeeeeeee jump!" He said that he was overcome with terror. Yet he got a second chance *(life is good about giving us second chances!),* and he said that he did the *hardest* thing he had ever done in his life . . . he let go! And when he did, sheer terror turned to sheer joy!

As soon as I read that part, I thought about how often I had been afraid to let go in my life—of a relationship that had not been working for a long time, of a job I didn't like, of beliefs that didn't work for me anymore, and so on. I remembered the times when I finally did have the courage and faith to let go (often after much pain and suffering), that everything had always worked out, and had usually worked out even better than I could have imagined.

Suddenly, I knew I *had to* take that literal leap of faith! I had to have the experience of sheer terror turning to sheer joy! And once I made that clear decision and commitment, things started falling into place for me to make it happen.

I had heard that it cost $80 to do the bungee jump. Since I had recently taken a leap of faith and quit my job just 7 years short of full retirement to go out on my own, I didn't feel that I had that extra money to spend. Then I remembered what one of my teachers (Edwene Gaines, a Unity minister) had taught me—our job is to ask for what we want, choose to believe, then leave the "how to" up to God. We simply let go and let God. God is our Source and the "how to" is God's business. OK, then—I knew that somehow I would find a way to do this.

I happened to mention it to my son who then said that my son-in-law was thinking of doing this also. I immediately called my son-in-law, and he told me that he was indeed going and had some friends who wanted to go, too. He said my son and I were welcome to come along. Wow! Now I had some people to go with!

I was still concerned about the money, and we soon heard that the cost had been cut to $40! (*Now, I don't know if that had anything to do with an incident that I read about in the newspaper the day before where a man in California was killed bungee jumping, but for whatever reason the price had been cut in half!*)

So my son-in-law (a police officer), two of his buddies (one a police officer), my son and I all decided to go take this leap. (*I found out later that my son-in-law's police buddy said to him, "Aw, man! Why'd you invite her? If she jumps, we've got to jump, or we can't show up at the station again!*)

We met at the fairgrounds the next day. As we walked in, we could see a big crane lifting a platform high into the air with a potential jumper in it, and I started feeling excited! As we got closer, I felt that excitement change to fear. But I was there now, and I wasn't going to let fear stop me.

We got in the short line of people waiting to jump. The first thing we had to do was sign a two-page list stating things that could go wrong and waive the company of any liability by signing it. There were over a dozen paragraphs to be read and initialed. I thought, "There's no way I am going to read all this and put fear into my mind!" So I initialed every paragraph, signed the form without reading it, and handed it back. (*God is my Source. I am always safe.*)

As we waited for our turns, I watched people ahead of me checking and double checking the straps being buckled onto their ankles, asking questions like "Has this ever broken?" and "Have you ever seen anyone get killed?" (*Breathe, Judee!*)

I reminded myself that my faith was not in the bungee cord, the ankle straps, or the reliability of the crew. My faith was in God. (*Oh, by the way, this was before bungee jumping was regulated in Florida following some deaths. After regulation, ankle straps could no longer be used—they used seat harnesses instead—and the height was lowered.*)

I watched a couple of people go up, freeze with fear, and come back down in the cage. I noticed that both of them kept looking down. (*Note to self: Do NOT look down!*)

Suddenly it was my turn to get my ankles strapped to the bungee cord. (I went first in our little group—I wanted to get it over with before fear had a chance to take over!) The gate to the platform opened and the jump master invited me to step in. I hobbled over, gulped, and stepped in. My heart was pounding so hard I was sure people could see it. I kept telling myself, "God is protecting me. I am safe."

The jump master asked me my name and introduced himself as Jim. He calmly explained to me what was going to happen. My heart continued pounding wildly, yet I knew I could *not* let fear take over.

The platform was slowly lifted into the air. I focused my full attention on Jim, looking directly at his face and listening intently to his words, yet vaguely aware of being lifted higher and higher.

Jim said, "Judee, when I say '3, 2, 1, bungee jump,' I want you to not even think about it—just let go and jump!" At that moment, I made the 100% commitment to myself that I would jump as soon as he said that—no matter what!

When we reached a height equivalent to a 12-story building, the cage stopped. Jim opened a small gate, told me to step onto a tiny platform, just big enough for my two feet, and to hold onto the handrails. I did as he instructed staring straight ahead. I admit I made one very *quick* glance down, immediately knowing that was *not* the thing to do!

Then Jim called out, "3, 2, 1 . . . bungeeeeee jump!" My commitment kicked in for me (because I felt numb with fear), and sure enough—I let go, closing my eyes and automatically extending my arms out to my sides, letting myself simply fall forward. (*I did a graceful swan dive, although it was an unconscious act. I only know this because I got a video of my jump.*)

The reporter was right! When I let go, sheer terror turned to sheer joy! What a feeling of elation and aliveness! Talk about feeling high on life! Wow, wow, wow!

When I got back on the ground, my whole body was trembling, yet I felt great! I did it—I really did it! I then watched each of the guys go . . . they *had to* go after I did it!

When I got in bed that night, I realized the amazing spiritual lessons I had learned from this experience: the joy of taking a leap of faith—successfully, the power to refuse to let fear stay in my thoughts, the power of having absolute focus on what I wanted, the power of 100% commitment (I don't think could have done it with 98%!), and the power in letting go. I thought of how I could apply what I learned to any and all areas of my life where I found myself afraid to let go . . . or where I was letting fear stop me from doing something I wanted to do. I fell asleep overflowing with appreciation that I had done this thing (and with no thoughts of *ever* doing it again).

And, when I woke up the next morning, a voice in my head said, "Judee, you weren't paying full attention yesterday. You had your eyes closed until the first bounce. You were half unconscious with fear and missed a lot of the joy there was to be had. Go back today and do it with your eyes open!"

Then a different voice, said, "Another $40! You need that to help pay bills."

I said to myself, "OK, do I believe that God is my Source— or not? If I think I can't afford $40, then I believe that I will not be provided with more money when I need it to pay bills. Is that where I want to place my faith? No way! For me to be in integrity with what I say I believe, then I've got to be OK with paying another $40."

So I went back by myself later that day. Before I got in line, I stood watching some people jump. A young couple was standing beside me also watching the jumpers. The young woman asked me if I was going to do it. I told her about my experience the day before and why I was back today. I asked her if she was going to do it, and she said, "No, way! I'm too scared, but my boyfriend is going to."

I got in line again. I still felt some fear, yet now I knew about the power of courage, faith, commitment, focus, and letting go. I went up and jumped again . . . this time with my eyes wide open! I felt even more joy and elation than the day before.

I realized how often I had missed out on experiencing the joy of the moment because I was feeling fear. I declared to myself right then and there my intention to pay attention more and more in life to each moment, to let go of fear thoughts when I noticed them coming in, and to live life to the fullest . . . as a wonderful daring adventure!

As I started to leave, I saw friends of mine who had been watching people jump, and they congratulated me, amazed that I had done it. Then as I walked on, I saw the young couple. The young woman called to me and said, "Guess what! I did it! I jumped, and it was all because of you!" Wow, another lesson learned for me! Just by living our lives authentically, we can make a big difference in others' lives, others that we might not even know. (*Thank you, God!*)

But, wait . . . God wasn't through with the blessings for me in this experience yet! The next day, a Sunday, I went to my Unity church feeling so grateful for my bungee jumping experience and what I had learned from it.

After the service, a friend walked up to me and handed me a folded check, telling me she had heard me speak at a Sunday service a few weeks back, had been inspired by what I had shared, and wanted to tithe to me. I was amazed and I thanked her, gave her a hug, and slipped the check into my pocket without looking at it.

Later as I was driving home, I remembered the check in my pocket. I felt so grateful to have received a tithe because I knew that was a sign that I had been a source of spiritual growth for my friend. It was the first time I had ever received a tithe, and it was based on the very first time I had ever spoken at a Unity church service. I took out the check and looked at it . . . my heart jumped, and then I laughed out loud!

My friend knew nothing about my bungee jump or about my concern for spending $40 twice. So . . . guess what the amount of the check was? Yes! $80! The exact amount I had spent on taking two leaps of faith! To me, that was God saying, "See, I told you that you could trust me!" My reaction was "Yes-s-s-s-ssss! Thank you, God!"

So from my bungee jumping adventure, I learned about and experienced the power of courage, faith, letting go, 100% commitment, total focus on my goal, and paying full attention in the moment. And the power of following my heart and trusting God as my Source. I also learned that, when I am being my authentic self and following my heart, I am a model of possibility for others.

I have used this experience over and over again as a touchstone in my life to help me move beyond fears that come up and to experience the joy of going for what I want . . . and getting it.

Bungee jumping may not be for you, yet I encourage you to use my experience as an inspiration to be true to yourself and go for what *you* want in *your* life. Whenever you feel fear overtaking your thoughts and stopping you from letting go of what is no longer for your good, or stopping you from going for what you want, just know that faith is a choice—and where you place that faith is a choice.

Now I want to tell you about an encounter I had several years after I had spoken about my bungee jump experience at my Unity church. A friend happened to run into me in a restaurant and said, "Judee, I want to tell you something. I heard you speak about your bungee jump at church awhile back . . . and I knew that I did not want to do that. But last summer, my husband and I went to the Grand Canyon on our vacation. He wanted me to go on the horseback ride down the canyon, and I told him, "No way!" because I was too scared. Then all of a sudden, I remembered your bungee jump, and I realized this was my "bungee jump! I thought to myself, 'If Judee could do it, I can do it!'" So I told my husband, 'Yes,' and we had the most wonderful time. Thank you so much!"

May my story inspire you to take *your* leap of faith, your version of my bungee jump, knowing that God is your Source and that you cannot fail when you step out on faith. I *know* your leap of faith will become your jump for joy! Enjoy this daring adventure called life . . .

About the Author

Judee Light is a speaker, teacher, author, editor, F.U.N. facilitator, and adventure lover with over 33 years' experience. She is a fourth generation Unity student and has been speaking at Unity churches for over 22 years. She is the author of the book, *When I Let Go and Let God.* You can find out more about her and what she is about at www.FeelingUpliftedNow.com (F.U.N.).

Fear - The Immobilizer!

Martha A. Sanchez

How many times have you had an exciting idea, then fear raised its head and squashed it? The fear of failure or the fear of success — yes, being successful can be scary too! During conversations with my Mommy to Mogul coaching clients, fear always comes up in one form or another. Many times you don't even recognize it. Fear can manifest itself through excuses that justify your reasons for not reaching for a goal or sabotaging yourself by your own negative thoughts.

Throughout my own career, fear has raised its head. Sometimes I too gave in to the fear. Then I realized that the fear emerged from my own self-doubt. And who controls that? I do! I decided I would not let fear control my mind.

How did I do this? Well, I separated myself from the situation and looked at it objectively. If I was helping someone in the same situation, what would I look for as a measure of their success? It may sound silly but sometimes we just have to get out of our own way.

Fear is just an emotion, and you give it power. I came up with a way to overcome my fears by applying my **RULE** strategy outlined below.

Regulate the negativity and self-doubt.

Unravel the real cause of the fear.

Look at the worst case scenarios, should things go wrong, and create a plan and alternate plan to mitigate them.

Evaluate, analyze and adjust your plan as needed.

By taking emotion out of the equation, you can analyze the situation and make plans.

This strategy was a result of conversations I had with homeless patients at a shelter. As the Director of Clinical Operations at a homeless shelter, I had various conversations with the residents while trying to provide them with resources for their future. One conversation was especially eye-opening. I will call this person John to protect his/her identity along with some of the details. The context of the conversation is accurate.

John was a Cuban Refugee who had been in the United States for less than 6 months, and like other residents of the homeless shelter, he had difficulty with money management and prioritization. This was affecting him dramatically to the point that he was considering returning to Cuba. This plan was incomprehensible to me as well as to the other staff members. Yet, when you looked at the circumstances, his confusion revolved around "having too many choices."

John had grown up in a culture where everything was decided for him, including what he studied at school. His food was predetermined and rationed – one week rice, another week potatoes, and once in a while meat — if he was lucky. He was appointed to a career based on the needs of the government, regardless of his desire or aptitude, and was forced to serve in the military. He was given a ticket to buy one item — shirt or pants. He was told where he could live. In essence, there was nothing for him to decide; it was all decided for him.

When he came to the United States, he had all these choices to make yet he had never developed the skills necessary to make them. As a result, he was not able to budget his money and he became homeless. He lived for each day, fearful that he would never get to enjoy some of the things he wanted.

As I thought about John's comments, my mind spun, making connections with other residents in similar circumstances. I thought of the mothers who gave their children soft drinks instead of milk, even though they were educated that it was not healthy for their children. When asked why, they said it was because they wanted them to be happy. I started asking more questions, and it dawned on me that John and the other residents were making choices based on fear. They were afraid they could not make it on their own. They all came from a world of control, poverty, violence and death. They just wanted to enjoy themselves while it lasted, because in their world, good things did not happen for people like them.

The reasons were always the same: self-doubt and the fear that they did not have the skills to survive. They were all caught in this vicious cycle, where they passed on this negativity and lack of hope from generation to generation. It had become part of their culture, spilling over from the effects of their past experiences.

You might be thinking that this doesn't apply to you, that these individuals have very different circumstances. Yet if you reflect on various instances in your life, you might find that although the circumstances may have been different, the feelings of self-doubt and fear were the same.

I had a client who had always wanted to start her own business. When I asked her why she had not moved forward with her dream, one thing was holding her back. She felt she was not experienced enough. Then I asked her about her current job and duties she handled there. She started going through a list of skills and responsibilities that were exactly the kinds of qualities needed for an entrepreneur. Next, she went through a list of skills that she didn't have but needed to start her business. I acknowledged those things as being valid concerns and I asked her how she would handle those issues if they arose in her current job. As the discussion progressed, I noticed that she felt more comfortable finding solutions when the business she talked about was *not* her own company. Does this sound familiar? How much easier is it for you to find solutions for someone else's issues than your own?

I asked my client why she could not apply these same solutions to her own business plan. Immediately, her eyes opened wide and I could almost see the light illuminating from her. It was clear that she was actually capable of handling a business. "But I don't have the money for these solutions," she said. So we looked at prioritizing her needs. What was essential to begin the business? What could wait until later? How could she generate income to help with those expenses? When she analyzed it in steps, it was less threatening and easier to handle.

Certain events have such a great significance. They leave a huge impression on our lives. There are two such events that I want to share with you. Over the years, I have found that these events helped me overcome my self-doubt. During my childhood, my family moved around often and friendships were hard to maintain. I moved from school district to school district until finally, I was in an elementary school for more than one year. I tried to make friends and even found this boy who I developed a crush on. I thought he was so handsome but he always paid attention to another girl who looked more like him. You see, I was the shortest one in the class; I wore glasses and because I was Hispanic, didn't look like everyone else. I settled for looking at him from afar. But, one day he started paying attention to me, and I was ecstatic. For four days, he talked to me every day and walked with me in the halls. On the fifth day, he asked if he could copy from my paper during an upcoming test because I was so smart. I didn't know what to say. I wanted to help him but I knew cheating was wrong. So, I told him I would help him study and he could copy my notes. He got very angry and said he didn't want to waste his time. Needless to say, he stopped talking to me. In fact, I became the butt of his jokes on many occasions. I felt very unattractive, became introverted and grew very distrustful of boys.

When I got an A on the test, I heard him say that boys didn't like girls who were smarter than them. I was too embarrassed to tell my mother how much his statement had hurt, so I just asked her if it was true that boys didn't like smart girls. Her comment was very profound. She said, "Only a boy who is insecure says something like that. And you should never let someone else's insecurity become yours." This was an AHA moment for me. Why was I allowing this person to make me feel unworthy? What this taught me was that although I may feel hurt by the words of others, I will not allow their words to define me. I have my own goals and dreams.

The second event involved my grandmother. She was a very smart woman who grew up on a ranch in Cuba in the

1920's and only had an elementary school education. She washed clothes by hand and ironed them with a metal iron heated on the stove. My grandmother was married at 16, had a child by 17 and divorced by 20. She moved away from her hometown, as a single parent, became an assistant to a local midwife and often delivered children on her own when the midwife was at another delivery. She was forced to leave her native country in order to escape Fidel Castro's communist regime, and come to the United States in 1966. Even though she was in her early 50's, she learned enough English to communicate effectively.

If you think that this woman was limited because of her age and education, you would be wrong. She was a cleaning woman in downtown Manhattan near the Empire State building, but she had a dream. She wanted to travel the world and learn about different cultures. Some people might think this was a pipe dream and that she could never afford to do this. Well, these people too would be wrong. She had a dream and she created a plan to make that dream come true. She put money aside for her travels and never let anything get in her way.

She had great determination to make that dream a reality regardless of the obstacles that got in the way. I remember an instance when I was about 5 or 6 years old and my grandmother was coming home from work. She had just gotten paid and cashed her check. While getting into the elevator of our apartment building in New York City, a man came in grabbed her purse and ran out. My petite grandmother (she was only 4' 11") ran after the man forcing him to run down the stairs. I remember my mother screaming, "Mom, stop! He could hurt you!" She chased him as far as she could and a police officer tried to help yet they were not able to catch him. If you think that put a damper on her dream, you underestimate her determination. She took on extra shifts to make up the difference in what she had lost. There was no way anyone was going to interfere with her plans. Before her death at the ripe age of 86, my grandmother had visited Rome, Spain, Ecuador, Jamaica, Mexico, and the Bahamas. I had the privilege of traveling with her to Canada when I was 12 years old.

My grandmother died the way she lived, on her own terms. She valued her independence and lived on her own, next to her sister. She did not want to be limited by any physical restrictions, and her biggest concern was to be immobilized and dependent on others. During the last two weeks of her life, both my grandmother and I knew her time was limited. She died as she wanted, in her bed as she slept. Although her passing was painful for all of us, it was a blessing for her. We found her in bed, looking at a picture of her mother with her right hand extended as if she was reaching for my great-grandmother's hand.

I learned a great deal from my grandmother. She was a modern woman born in very conservative times. She was sometimes an outcast because of her strength of character and her unwillingness to be belittled for her lack of education or for her background. I learned determination, persistence, planning and yes, the love of traveling from my grandmother. She taught me to do what I loved regardless of what others might think. And most importantly, she encouraged me to be true to myself and never let fear control my life.

As my life progressed, I have used the lessons I learned from my mother and grandmother to overcome obstacles throughout my career as a Nurse, Health Care Risk Manager, Hospital Administrator, Controller/CFO, CEO, wife and mother.

Now, as a speaker, business coach, radio personality, author and CEO of a business consulting firm, I continue to use my RULE method. My strategies and techniques are key to fulfilling my mission of taking women from Mommy to Mogul by taking their life off pause to build a successful business. Through my business coaching and as host of the Mommy to Mogul Radio Show, I focus on empowering women to build their business and become financially independent.

The show airs Tuesdays at 7:00PM EST and you can listen live at www.MommyToMogulShow.com.

About the Author

Martha A. Sanchez is a speaker, business coach, radio personality, author and CEO of MAS Universal LLC. Martha's mission is to take women from Mommy to Mogul by taking their life off pause to build a successful business.

Through her business coaching and her Mommy to Mogul Radio Show which airs Tuesdays at 7:00PM EST on MommyToMogulShow.com, Martha focuses on empowering women to build their business and become financially independent.

Martha has a Bachelor in Nursing and an MBA. She has worked as a Health Care Risk Manager, Hospital Administrator, Controller/CFO, and CEO.

Martha is successful in providing valuable seminars to large audiences as well as smaller groups for more personalized attention. Her diverse work experience results in workshops that provide participants with practical techniques they can use to improve their management, communication, and marketing skills.

For more information, or to contact Martha, visit her website www.MarthaASanchez.com. Or if you are thinking of building a business and feeling overwhelmed or don't know where to begin just check out Martha A. Sanchez's **Mommy to Mogul Entrepreneur's Game Plan©.** It will give you a 7-step plan to help you start and energize your business! Take action and get an easy step-by-step roadmap that you can start using to build your business and live the life you dream of! Go NOW to

http://MarthaASanchez.com/Plan/

Words Can Change Your Life

Joanne Massey-Dean

There are many ways to change your life. The easiest and fastest way that I have found is to simply change your words. It is so powerful, yet many people are not aware that their choice in words can make or break their day, their conversations, their relationships and the way they feel about themselves. My specialty is improving women's self-esteem. One of the first things I work with women on is changing their words. The words that you say in your daily life and the words that you say to yourself, consciously and unconsciously, make a big difference in the results you get.

We all need to understand that our "self-talk" produces 100% of our results. If you are talking down to yourself and others, if you are frequently thinking about what can go wrong, that is what you attract in your life and that will also lower your self-esteem. For example if you are running late for an appointment, thinking about how late you are, thinking about getting slowed down by traffic, guess what happens....you get held up by traffic. This can cause a downward spiral. In the opposite scenario, you are still running late; however, this time, you bring a sense of gratitude to the situation. You are grateful that you are on your way to your appointment. You get to your first light and it is green, you feel gratitude for that green light and the rest of the trip goes well, because you are grateful, so you then attract more things to be grateful for. It is magical. Try it the next time you are not leaving as early as you wanted to.

What you say or think about others gets interpreted by your unconscious mind as what you say or think about yourself. Your unconscious mind thinks that what you are saying about others is actually being said about yourself. So when you say, for example, "What is wrong with her?" or "She looks awful," your unconscious mind interprets that as there being something wrong with you or that you look awful. So, what if you thought and said only positive statements? The same holds true. When you say or think, "What an amazing woman" or "She really looks good tonight," your mind reflects back to you that you are amazing and you really look good.

This happens in other areas of our lives as well. Your mind creates pictures of the words that you use. So are you creating the outcome that you truly desire? Are you using words that will improve your life and your self esteem? Or are the words you are using destined to lower it?

I learned from Dr. Yvonne Oswald that there are high energy and low energy words. The high energy words empower you and the low energy words take that power away. Our brain works like a search engine does on the internet. It looks for the words we are using. It does not, however, recognize words like "not" and "don't". For example, if I said, "Do not think about the pink elephant in the tree," your mind immediately thinks about the pink elephant in the tree. So by saying, "Don't worry," our mind hears worry and we start to worry. When someone says, "Thank-you" and you reply, "No problem" your mind is thinking there is a problem. If someone asks you how you are and you say, "Not bad" your mind hears "bad." Try changing your words. "You are welcome" or "I am good" are much better choices and will make you feel better as you say them. Try it. How are you? Now insert "Not bad." Notice the feeling you have in your body. Again...How are you? This time say, "I am good". Notice the feeling you have now. The feelings are quite different, aren't they? The power of your words is amazing, isn't it?

Avoid using low energy words such as: "problem," "difficult," "worry" and "hard". You can replace these with "interesting situation," "not easy" and "my pleasure." Also, add high energy words such as: "enthusiasm," "excitement," "success," "joy," "laughter," "gratitude," "delight" and "fulfillment." These words have a high impact. They will create a positive path and illuminate the way to a positively amazing future.

Another word to eliminate is "but". Replace it with "and" or simply drop the word and continue on with your statement. Any time you use "but" you negate everything that was said before that. "I like your dress, but you could have worn different shoes" gets replaced with, "I like your dress. What if next time you try black heels with it?" See the difference?

Try replacing "sorry" with "apologize". Sorry expresses regret for something, for example, the loss of a loved one or feeling sad about something. If you say or do something that another person takes offense to, try apologizing instead of being sorry. Let that person know that you accept responsibility for your actions, apologize for your actions and then state an alternative action for the future. For example: You are late for an appointment. Being sorry, you would say, "Sorry I am late, the traffic was really bad." Or you can apologize. "I apologize for being late; I know this really puts you off schedule for the rest of the day. In the future I will leave earlier to avoid unexpected delays along the way." In the latter, you accept responsibility, and the other person will really believe that you will do better in the future.

Now, let's replace the word "try". To try to do something means you will fail. Basically, you can do or do not, there really is no try. If I ask my husband to call me to remind me about an appointment and he replies, "I will try," do you really think I can depend on him to call me? No. I will set my alarm. On the other hand, if he says, "Yes, I will do that," I know he will. To try shows no real commitment. It is an uncertainty, and there is no effort being made by the person who is "trying." When you say to yourself that you will "try" to release weight, feel better about yourself, act with more confidence, or do better at work, chances are you will not succeed. If you just state that you *will* release weight, *will* feel better about yourself, *will* act with more confidence and *will* do better at work, then you will succeed. It is all in the word that you say to yourself; eliminate "try" and just "do."

What about words such as "should," "have to," got to"? These words make us feel like we have to do something even if we don't want to. "I have to go to work." "I should write a book." "I've got to go to a networking meeting." What feelings do you get when you say or read these statements? I get a feeling of obligation, and not necessarily a good one. I also feel anxiety and maybe even overwhelm. These are words our parents used when we were children. "You have to clean your room." "You should be nice to your brother." "You've got to do your homework." These are parental words and they do not make us feel like we really want to do the action attached to them. Replace these words with words such as "get to," "am able to" or "choose to." Look at and feel the difference. "I get to go to work today." "I am able to write a book." "I choose to go to a networking event today."

I now ask you, what words are *you* using every day? What are you saying to yourself? What are you saying about others? Remember the unconscious mind cannot tell the difference between what you are saying about others and what you are saying about yourself. It thinks you are always talking about yourself.

My challenge to each of you is to focus on one high energy word a day, and use that word as much as you can. At the same time eliminate one low energy word. See how your life changes, see how your self esteem increases and see how many positive things come your way. High energy words include: "Beautiful," "Believe," "Choose," "Dream," "Easy," "Energy," "Feel," "Free," "Funny," "Happy," "Money," "Please," "Positive," "Success," "Thanks" and "Improve".

Low energy words include: "Afraid," "Anger," "Broke," "Cheap," "Control," "Difficult," "Disease," "Doubt," "Expensive," "Failure," "Fear," "Forgot," "Guilt," "Hard," "Idiot," "Loser," "Mean," "Reaction," "Sad," "Sick," "Stupid" and "Worry."

I promise you that if you change your words, you will change your life!

I was introduced to this concept when I attended an annual WPN Un-conference and heard Dr. Yvonne Oswald speak. I was intrigued; I bought her book and signed up for her NLP certification class. I began noticing a lot more positive events and people in my life when I changed my words and thoughts. The NLP techniques that I learned were amazing at getting past the feeling that "I did not deserve" to succeed. When Dr. Yvonne announced that she was returning to Ft. Lauderdale to teach a Hypnosis Certification class, I signed up immediately. If this woman was teaching and using this technique also, then I knew it was for me.

I had a private session with Dr. Yvonne and was able to break through a lot of barriers. She helped me to believe in myself, trust myself and reassured me that I was a wonderful person. After my session with her, I immediately started hearing people say that I glowed, that I looked happier and that I had an appearance of pride. Dr. Yvonne has changed my life and I am so happy that I learned her techniques, so that I can change the lives of others.

About the Author

Joanne Massey-Dean has always had a passion for helping other women. With over 25 years as an RN, she has been educating people on how to be healthier most of her adult life. Joanne has recently begun focusing on emotional health by supporting women in the process of increasing their self-esteem. She incorporates NLP (Neuro Linguistic Programming) and Clinical Hypnosis to assist others in getting past the blocks that are stopping them from being the best they can be in every aspect of their lives. With Joanne's expertise, and the techniques that she uses, the women who work with her Live Their Ultimate Lives, Now.

Connect with Joanne via email at Joanne@LiveYourUltimateLifeNow.com,
Phone or text 954-562-8128 or go on her website http://LiveYourUltimateLifeNow.com.

Facing Death: Lessons in Living

Barbara Gruber

Who would have known that the conversations and intimate moments that I shared with my dying Mother and Grandmother would provide me with perfect advice and lessons that would sustain and carry me through my own bald-headed encounter with ovarian cancer? By watching and listening carefully to the words, attitudes and actions of these two remarkable women, I found myself learning how to emulate grace under fire.

That fire began for us when my Dad's company transferred him from our lifelong home in the Chicago area to a fledgling South Florida territory. Mom looked forward to this adventure, although she wasn't feeling her best. We knew that her heart was hurting, since she lamented leaving our home and displacing my older brother while he was serving in Vietnam. "We have taken away Bill's home at a critical time in his life and he has lost that presence of a safe harbor." I reassured Mom with the old adage that home is where the heart is, "You have built a beautifully crafted haven in all our thoughts and hearts and Bill will feel that love." She understood, saying, "Your life will be whatever you place in your heart and mind."

Shortly after we arrived in Florida, Mom became seriously ill and was diagnosed with cancer of the bone marrow, known as multiple myeloma. At that time, the disease was considered fatal and the local oncologist predicted that she would have less than a year. Dad, in his broken-heartedness, tried to manage Mom's health and deny the reality of the verdict. She said, "I knew something was very wrong. You have to die from something sometime. I just hoped that I would not have to face this in my 40's." Mom's bold spirit and positive daily affirmations allowed her to live almost six years after that doctor's gloomy prognosis. She was teaching me that we should never let something or someone else dictate or limit the outcomes of our lives.

Mom was especially worried since my younger brother, Jim, was still in grade school. She grieved that she would not see him graduate high school and college and that she would be unable to support him or guide him through the milestones in his life. Mom's priority and treasure was her family, with the children as the shining stars. "Children are remarkable and have so much to teach us. Watch them carefully as they navigate through life, and let their wonder and joy rejuvenate you."

Mom was passionate about sharing her love for others through cooking. After her diagnosis, she would often stay up late at night reading cookbooks with a classic old movie on TV for company. She derived pleasure and inspiration looking for ways to create new and tasty delights. Dad had different ideas for Mom. He wanted her to follow a strict diet in an effort to cure her cancer, starting with eating handfuls of bitter tasting, supposedly healing, apricot pits. Good naturedly, Mom would oblige and adhere to the limiting diet plan when Dad was home. When she grocery shopped, she excitedly inspected all the luscious bakery goods on view in the glass display. "This is just like life, you must savor each present moment," and then she would go on to choose only one tempting treat. After arriving home, she would slowly consume her chosen pastry, and then put the bakery bag on the bottom of the garbage container so as not to alert Dad. One time when Mom was having difficulty walking, I aided and abetted her by sneaking her a morsel of cookie from the box of macaroons that Dad had brought home for his dessert. I succeeded on my first secret mission, but was caught on my second cookie maneuver. General Dad barked out to the troops, "What are you two doing? That's not part of the diet". He shook his head, but a smile crept up to the corners of his mouth. Mom said, "Life is give and take, and sometimes when you feel your life is taking too much, you should just think of the ways that your giving can replenish you."

Mom accepted Dad's restrictions and Dad allowed for Mom's needs. They both remained flexible to the dictates of the disease process just as they had been flexible to the give and take in marriage. Dad was still working full time during the day, working from home when he was able. He also took care of Mom through the night when she was confined to a hospital bed in the living room. The only disagreement my parents had throughout these challenging years was who would take better care of whom. Mom would say, "Thank you, you do so much for me. I could barely do half of all those things to care for you." Dad would say, "Oh, no, if the situation were reversed you would do more for me than I am doing for you." "No, I couldn't." "Yes, you would." "I couldn't." "You would."

Linked in with Mom's kind heart was her platform of no complaining. She experienced severe pain from the disease, the radiation and the chemo medications. Mom also knew she was losing the fight for her life. Still she never grumbled, protested or even uttered a harsh word. Whenever a sensation of pain would grab her, she would quickly monitor her verbal output and facial expressions to 'put on a happy face' or 'put your best foot forward.' As far back as I can remember, Mom's favorite 'bad' phrase to exclaim was "crumble burger!" using this expression when situations were not going as hoped. Just like eating a crumbling Sloppy Joe, this term aptly described many a loosely laid plan falling apart into a messy aftermath. And, with Mom's love of food, this expression probably had a hidden significance. Mom said, "Many a fabulous recipe for food or life requires us to add ingredients of which we may not be found. And we sometimes need to remove tidbits that we love, because they don't add the right flavor to the dish."

And just as Mom was, so was Grandma. Mom had learned her lessons from a great and noble teacher. Grandma was kindness personified and never used discouraging words or negative comments towards anyone or anything. "Never say anything you would not want to hear." There was a sound that Grandma made when life's challenges pressed on her boundaries of peaceful existence. The musical lilt of her sighed 'ho-ho' was not an evocative expression of Santa. This gentle sound conveyed Grandma's philosophies, "It may not seem this way now; however, if you keep going, everything will work out" and "You must accept everything as it is and keep moving forward" and "It's their prerogative to be that way, however you should choose not to let anyone or anything effect you negatively."

With a mighty ho-ho, Grandma accepted and hid her ovarian cancer from us, remaining upbeat, active and independent until she was hospitalized for the last three weeks of life. Here is where her uplifting nature shined the brightest. She also suffered from congestive heart failure, although you could argue that she never "suffered" since she never complained and never let this challenge stop her from handling all of her daily chores especially going on the retirement bus to get groceries for Sunday dinner, a family ritual that never varied. You were invited to arrive at noon (3 pm if the Dolphins were playing in the late game) if you could, and no worries if you could not or if you had to eat and run. As you would prepare to lift the first fork full of savory roast stuffed chicken or juicy pork loin to your mouth, there would suddenly appear at each seat an individual "to go" bag with another full portion of that day's glorious homemade dinner. "You can never pass around too much love or kindness."

Then the heat got turned up in my life. Having experienced both parents and grandmothers dying of complications from cancer, I always knew that there might be a time that I would have to face this opponent later in life. But never did I even consider that it would happen barely past 50. I have always tried to stay healthy by running five to six days a week, following a good diet and taking vitamins. OK, I'll admit that I did slip from time to time having my own "macaroon moments." My friend, Thais, loves to say, "We are like apples, we look good from the outside. It's not 'til you cut us open that the true picture emerges." I decided that when I was cut open, what would emerge was a positive, joyful attitude coupled with a sense of humor. So, in January 2005, I was led into the testing grounds.

Our son, Paul, was still in grade school, so I knew exactly how Mom had felt about leaving my brother while he was so young. Mom's words rang in my mind, "You have to die from something," but I wasn't quite ready to die just yet. In the secret style of Grandma, I did not want to tell my husband, Richard, and disrupt his tax season. I had to tell someone, so my sole confidant became my younger brother, Jim. Until the diagnosis of my trusted doctor was confirmed, I spent several days outwardly smiling, silently crying and learning how to strengthen my reserve. God granted me the inner peace that surpasses all understanding, which was profoundly helpful when one pre-surgical procedure went awry. I ended up spending several extra days in the hospital before surgery. I was blessed with being a patient in the hospital that was my work place for twenty years and a constant stream of old friends and new friends came in for laughter, hugs and prayers. My biggest concern during this time was to make sure that all of my visitors would leave me feeling optimistic and upbeat! A new doctor brought in on my case remarked that I had the best attitude of any patient he had witnessed in his thirty years of practice. His compliment, combined with God's watchful eye, spurned me on to even greater heights. I began to positively reframe the cancer and my life. A good field test for my new skill set came quickly, since I had to remain on IVs for eight days. I thought of Mom and knew there would be a future time when I could skip down the bakery aisle of goodies and experience a more pleasant 'treat.' For now, I could only covet my roommate's bright yellow Jell-O.

Chemo started three weeks after surgery. During those three weeks I, as a runner, found it amazingly cathartic to walk at least a mile every day. I had just successfully squelched the burning embers of complete hair loss 13 days after my first chemo treatment. I give great credit to many women who go out 'au natural.' No offense to the handsome men on both sides of my family, but I looked like my departed Dad from the side view and Uncle Bob from the front. Therefore, I opted to wear a soft hat with a long flowing scarf tied around the brim to hang down and give me a Lady Godiva air. Unfortunately, after my third treatment I injured my back. With Richard working long hours during tax season, I did not want to disturb him at night. At 4'10" pulling down the Murphy Bed in the guest room was a task that sheared part of my disc. After that, I could only say that sleep is vastly overrated, since I sure wasn't getting any. The sciatic nerve down my whole left leg, which poked fun at me throughout the day, really came out to play at night. When the best of spirit and the constant repetitive chant, "I feel great!" could no longer offset the agony, I finally agreed to take pain medication. A dose could secure me about two hours sleep, so I often became greedy, taking a second night-time tablet when I awoke in the wee hours of the morning. That left me with 20 hours a day to talk to God and really hone Mom and Grandma's motivational skills. I learned that my focus and my words became my pervasive reality, one that I was literally recreating every few minutes. I used "I'm doing great", "All is well", "oh, crumple burger" and "ho-ho". Bible verses empowered me, especially one that said 'my grace is sufficient for you, for my power is made perfect in weaknesses.' When situations got really tough, I would repeat these strengthening words multiple times as a mantra, "your grace is sufficient for me, your grace IS sufficient for me," until the power of this phrase would uplift me. As my friend Craig always reminds me, "This too shall pass." And pass it did, when three weeks to the day after my last chemotherapy treatment I had surgery on my back to correct the disc!

Barbara's Little Bits of Action for
Living Your Best Life:

SET PRIORITIES

Dig deep, and follow your driving passions. Set those passions as priorities for your life, and then follow that list with both your mind and your heart. One day, when I was having a challenging moment, my son Paul held out his arms to hug me. "Mom, you need a heart charge." How perceptive of him, since hugs do help and revitalize you. To this day, I whole-heartedly embrace others both physically and mentally.

BE FLEXIBLE

Be willing to be flexible. Just as life requires that you take responsibility to sculpt and form your future, you must also allow yourself to be shaped and molded by your experiences. You have to take paths that challenge your growth and you need to release comfortable habits that may be restricting that very growth. The warming fires returned again a few years ago when I began experiencing sciatic nerve pain that gave me daily companionship only when sitting or lying down. Hey, who could complain, I'm still walking. Believing that I had exacerbated the site of my back surgery, I muddled through for 18 months and finally made an appointment with the doctor just in case. My neurosurgeon had warned me that that if I reinjured the area there may be little that could be done to correct the damage. The scan showed that I needed double hip replacement. That was over a year ago and losing my physical flexibility during that year has become a huge and humbling lesson for me. Actually the lack of flexibility has made me realize the great privilege I once had of tying my shoes, cutting my toenails and walking without a cane.

It should be noted that my faith has led me to try alternative methods and prayer one last time, before facing the hip clipping machinery. The defining moment that sealed the deal for putting off the procedure was when the doctor said that the implants would not bring me from four foot ten to the world of five footers. Well, a girl can dream. I will never know if this disorder was accelerated by chemotherapy, unfriendly genes and/or 35 years of having my running shoes hit the pavement or soft sand every day. Either way, my running career was over after back surgery and the days of flexible hips are, at least for now, behind me. This latest challenge has stoked the fires in all the other areas of my life.

USE DISCERNMENT

Well meaning people will give well-meaning advice concerning your life and their thoughts on the best ways for you to live that life. Do not get overwhelmed when you are bombarded with "too much information" in the form of conflicting opinions and ideas. When I went through cancer and chemo, I was the regular recipient of all kinds of appealing ideas on how to achieve wellness: "Drink a mixture of fresh juiced fruits and veggies" "Juice veggies only, don't mix fruits" "Don't just juice, you need pulp, too" and "Don't consume any raw produce because you are especially susceptible to the bacteria." As long as I was willing to do everything and anything, I could follow everybody's advice. The preceding four ideas could all be thrown into a pot to make a tasty soup!

I learned that when unsure of the correct direction, seek advice, use your instincts, take action and ask the Almighty to guide you through each step. We can be challenged if we do not carefully monitor the condition of our body, mind and spirit. Our attitudes, word choices and expressions reveal the way the world will view us. Studies have proven that your mind takes cues from your facial expressions. I decided that whatever look you wear on your face is the garment that wraps your mind, so why not be in fashion with a smile.

LOOK FOR THE BEST

Remember, in conversations often the important part is not always stated in words. There are inferred meanings, descriptive emotions and telltale attitudes imparted in the way we deliver the message. Besides gluing a smile to my face, I try to respond to others in an enthusiastic manner using upbeat words. With so many people asking how I'm doing, I have upgraded "I'm great" to "Terrific" or "Doing fabulously." I often notice people smiling back, yet with a quizzical look on their face as their eyes quickly gaze down at my cane. I am fortunate to have this experience, which I view as more great chapters for the book. The bottom line for me is to follow my beloved role models, Mom and Grandma. They impressed upon me the true value in searching for the brightest outlook in every situation. I am very much defined by something my husband Richard often says: "You are the person who can find the silver lining in every garbage can."

About the Author

Barbara Gruber, an Occupational Therapist, holds a Masters in Healthcare Management. She worked in mental healthcare for over 30 years, also doing home therapy with stroke patients. When Barbara had her son late in life, she entered her most rewarding career. From an early age, she has been smiling, and urging people to "Live your best life". She always brings her positive attitude, sense of humor and cheerful countenance, specializing in unearthing the bright side in everything.

Barbara practices Healing Touch, Energy Medicine and Low-Level Laser Therapy. Her Life Coaching practice is the perfect complement to her healthcare devotion. By helping others redefine and promote their changing roles in career, life-purpose, health status and relationships, Barbara motivates them to flourish and live their optimal life.

She is currently writing her book, in which she shares a series of encouraging stories to uplift and comfort people whose lives have been touched by cancer.

This is one of those stories.

Connect with Barbara at: barbarajgruber@gmail.com

Something's Got to Change!

Susan Wiener

In my experience the journey usually begins in a moment of Frustration or Desperation when you say, "I can't take it anymore, something's got to change!"

Can you remember a time in your life like that? A time when you said, "I can't take it anymore," and you went in search of a solution? I can remember several times in my life and I bet you can, too.

The last time for me was when my Mom died after I had been her caretaker for the last 14 months of her life.

For years, my Mom suffered from several chronic conditions including COPD and heart problems. When it came time for her to retire, my sisters and I attempted to convince her to move to Florida so she could be close to us and she refused. Despite her health issues, she chose to move to her dream location and live her dream life in Las Vegas on the opposite side of the country from me and my two sisters. She never let her "conditions" stop her from doing the things she loved. Then, when she was diagnosed with cancer, and as her health deteriorated, she began making more frequent trips to the hospital and rehab, and staying longer each time. At that time my sisters and I were running a very successful title company and my sisters took turns flying out to Vegas while I stayed behind and kept the business going.

On the last trip, my sister returned with the news that my Mom was only expected to live for three more weeks. We again explored the possibility of moving her to Florida and were told by the doctors that she was too frail and could not survive the trip. She was very weak and sleeping most of the time, fighting infections and fading away.

Hearing that news, I decided it was time for me to fly to Vegas for a last visit with her and say my goodbyes. To my surprise, when I arrived she woke up, sat up, perked up and over the next few days, had a "miraculous" recovery, getting stronger hour by hour and day by day. The doctors were astounded and told me that if we wanted to move her to do it now. And so we did, within 48 hours.

Flights and medical assistance were arranged, I packed a bag for her and we snuck out of the rehab and visited her favorite casinos and friends. Then we were off to Florida and she came to live with me. She spent the first few weeks complaining and expressing everything she "hated" about her new living situation. Things like on the drive home from the airport "There aren't even sidewalks here", entering her new room "I hate that color sheets", "It always rains here", etc. This was a sure sign she was feeling better. And, as the weeks passed and she was feeling better and better, she began to adapt to her new environment and embrace all the good in this new chapter of her life.

As with everything I do, I went "all in" and became an excellent caretaker for her (it became my full time job) and, as a result, she experienced a "rich" 14 months being surrounded and supported by family, visiting our local casinos and playing in card games with no trips to the hospital. She died in peace and smiling. I had no regrets.

A few weeks after her death (and the loss of my full time job and purpose), I began to feel "lost" and incapable of doing anything well. I had no idea what to do or pursue and got depressed and immobilized. In a moment of desperation, feeling "I couldn't take it anymore," I went in search of a solution. Things had to change.

Having heard about a free tele-class led by Gloria Ramirez, I dialed in and stayed on the line, despite the fact that I had difficulty hearing and could only really grasp a portion of what she was saying. What I did hear and understand was that I needed to remember who I was at the core and reconnect with that first, and in that moment I began to find myself again.

In the days and weeks to follow, my full time job became rediscovering who I really was – what made me feel good - what made me happy. I listened to and read as much as I could on the subject and spent quiet time searching for answers. I started writing a daily gratitude list of at least ten things I was grateful for in my life and having conversations with myself that really mattered, focusing on all the good in my life. And I began to see and appreciate how really blessed I am. From there I began to journal, opening up the space for my core feelings and thoughts to flow again.

Through this process I found I was able to shift my energy from "fearful and anxious" to "faith-filled and excited" – not an easy job in the beginning. Each day, I added something to my daily process. I came up with five basic sentences that I required myself to complete before tackling my seemingly overwhelming "To Do" list and found that, in doing so, the list was much easier to handle and I accomplished much more in less time with a lot less stress.

Here are the 5 sentences:

1 - I'm so happy and grateful for…

2 - I'm excited about…

3 - I see myself…

4 - I'm expecting…

5 - I'm passionate about and committed to…

As time went on, I learned to add "I'm feeling" to the sentences and as I did so, they became much more powerful. Then I discovered that by adding "as a result of" at the beginning or end of the sentences, they took on yet another dimension. For example, "I'm expecting everything to flow smoothly today as a result of feeling centered, peace filled and loving."

Through this process, I also rediscovered and clearly defined what my special "gift" was…the gift of encouragement. I realized my greatest joy has always come as a result of encouraging every person I connect with to feel better about themselves, their situation and their life. I began "consciously" finding ways to do that and ways to reach more people. And my new career was born. I was excited again about my life, feeling happy, grateful, enthused and peaceful. Today I am happy to say that I have developed many programs and have assisted hundreds of people in quickly "transitioning" when they have the feeling "I can't take it anymore, something's got to change."

My daily habits now include at least 15 minutes of spiritual exercise every morning. I have developed the habit of creating my "To Be" list before tackling my "To Do" list and have discovered that this practice results in a much more peaceful, powerful, productive, prosperous day!

I share this story with you in the hope that the next time you are feeling "I can't take it anymore... something's got to change" you can quickly find a solution.

About the Author

CeCe Espeut Photography & Video

Susan Wiener, aka "The Luminary," is the COO and Co-Founder of Women's Prosperity Network, LLC. Susan has had a long and successful career in leadership and management for large corporations and small businesses. Her many talents and gifts include her ability to provide inspiration, guidance, encouragement and support to individuals on the path to creating a more fulfilling, abundant life, as well as her hands-on skill to solve challenges with creative, simple, effective solutions. She has had the entrepreneurial spirit since the 1980's and has led several organizations. She is also the co-owner of an Auto Brokerage firm that makes the car buying experience easy for the consumer while saving money on the purchase.

For more information about Susan and/or Women's Prosperity Network or connection with her go to http://wpnglobal.com/about or email susan@womensprosperitynetwork.com.

A Mother's Gift

Jan Kinder

What if someone who had been your total support system all of your life was no longer there?

September 23, 2009 was a very beautiful and most heart-wrenching day, the day my life would be forever changed. On that Wednesday afternoon, I had the honor of helping my mother transition and cross over. The sudden onset of my mother's illness and the unfortunate set of circumstances that ended her life within two weeks was quite a shock, to say the least. Just three weeks before, we were at a restaurant having dinner together.

The voyage I was to embark upon had already set sail. A new journey of courage, strength, taking risks, trusting my intuition, and having faith in divine intervention had already launched, unbeknownst to me. It began with the rocky waters surrounding my mother's hospitalization.

During Mom's two-week hospital stay, I gathered up my inner resources to stay centered and resilient for her. It was my privilege to care for her. I needed to, and wanted to be mother's strength, loving support and voice. Nothing else was more important to me. Lying in that hospital bed was the person closest to me, my greatest pillar of strength and now she was vulnerable. She was unable to speak due to being intubated and in a great deal of pain and filled with fear. She wanted to pull through and live. A multitude of what I will call "a disturbing and unfortunate turn of events" beckoned my full attention and perseverance in seeking the best care possible for her.

When she unexpectedly suffered what the doctors called a catastrophic stroke, I honored my mother's wishes to not be on life support. On her final day, the doctors explained that she was in a vegetative state, yet not brain dead. As a nurse, I knew this meant on some level she was aware. When the breathing tube was removed, she continued to breathe on her own. The doctors kept her medicated and comfortable.

As the time of her departure grew near, her life essence had already begun to leave her body. Mom and I had made a promise years ago that I would be there to help her when it was her time to pass. Having experienced my own near death years ago, I trusted that my heart and spirit would lead me.

The most loving gesture I could do for mom was to encourage her to keep rising, moving towards the light and to go with the angels. Though selfishly I wanted more time with her, the words, spoken from my heart, reassured her it was okay to go. I told her our family would be all right. Then, I expressed how much I loved her and kissed her on her forehead.

When her vital signs on the hospital monitor were low, I sang "Amazing Grace" and as my song came to an end, I noticed her blood pressure and heart rate on the monitors had increased to normal levels. It was wonderful to know my mother had heard me and responded to me in this way. I wondered though, if engaging her was keeping her here, calling her back, so I whispered the hardest words I've ever had to say, "I love you and will stay with you, but will no longer speak to you on this level. It's time for you to go. Your mother's waiting for you. Good bye Mommy." Eight minutes later, her torment was over and she peacefully ascended with the angels.

With tear-filled eyes, gratitude comforted me. She was everything I could ask for in a mother. We spoke everyday; sharing our stories and insights. It was only after she was gone that I came to realize just how much I actually relied on her for her intuitive guidance. The epitome of unconditional love, she was a spiritually aligned healer and nurse, embracing life with youthful enthusiasm and joy. She would surely live on and shine in the hearts of so many who she so graciously touched.

However, the myriad of questions that arose during her hospitalization still flooded my mind. Why did it happen? Could they have done more for her? Could I have done more? The many unanswerable whys, what if's and should have's lingered inside of me for many months.

After the funeral, I completely let down my "persona of having it all together" and I collapsed. The women in my life were and are loving, caring and supportive. I am blessed to have them. At the same time, I was asking myself, "what am I going to do?" My mom, best friend and mentor, was no longer here. Our daily chats and fun times together were now a thing of the past. I felt lost and alone. The proverbial rug had been pulled out from under me. Suddenly, nothing made sense.

I felt like a part of me died with her. In the middle of one sleepless night, it hit me. There was, indeed, a piece of me that died with her. I wept uncontrollably for that missing part. I was mourning the loss of my dependence on her and the many roles she played in my life. Yet, I did not see it as dependence. In my mind and heart, she was the one I shared my everyday life with. The significant choices I made in life, we made together. This was to change. No longer would I be able to "bounce things off her." No longer would I hear her words of encouragement and trust, at least not on the physical level. I knew it was my turn to trust myself to do what she had done for and with me, on my own. But, how?

Things that once held meaning were no longer important. Or so it seemed. In many ways, I was numb to living beyond the parameters of the world now past; the world that I had on this earth with my mother. I was having difficulty functioning. All I wanted to do was sort through her belongings, try on her clothes, sleep in her bed and connect with her friends. I wanted to smell her scent and to feel her essence around me. I wanted to absorb her into every cell, into the very core of my being, so I would never forget. I took up residency in my mother's house for the next two and a half months while I prepared her estate.

Even though I had been meditating most of my life, the thought of meditation escaped me. I did not want to be quiet, did not want to close my eyes. Not then. The images of my mother's painful and frightening misfortune haunted me. I was not finished being angry. My heart ached for mom. I felt compassion and gave myself permission to grieve for as long as I needed.

Two months after mom's passing, I was once again meditating and practicing self-care. I found it valuable to journal and talk about my experience with other motherless daughters for my own personal release and consolation. I made a conscious choice to begin to celebrate my mother's life with joy.

A new strength and mission was developing inside of me that would prepare and lead me through the next three and a half years of my journey. When I returned home to St. John, Virgin Islands, I needed to catch up with my work and home life. But, my daily life changed immediately. Once again, I was being called upon to help someone. Needless to say, I had a full plate. For the next twelve months I became the caregiver for a long-time colleague and friend. I was like a daughter to her, and she was a "mother figure" to me. As her time on this earth came to a close, I helped her to comfortably pass.

The inner strength I received to embrace this challenge was grounded in unconditional love and compassion. What I was capable of was to be revealed.

For brevity's sake, I will simply list the overlapping order of other events as they occurred. They would emotionally challenge me and, at the same time, guide me on my path:

- The passing of a cousin and two close friends.
- The selling of the house I designed, and helped to build. My hope was that this would be where I would retire.
- Closed my award winning mind-body-spirit wellness center.
- Resigned as executive director of St. John School of the Arts where I had been in various positions for 27 years.
- Moved to Florida but had no clue what was next.
- Relocated and built my new wellness center, which took a year.

- Became the primary caregiver for my husband after quadruple heart by-pass surgery.
- Opened the wellness center.
- Again, became the primary caregiver for my husband after his second quadruple heart by-pass surgeries within nine months.
- Stepped back onto my path fully.

The stronger I became, the more my awareness rose, showing me I needed to move forward. I was about to shake it all up. After I buried my elderly friend, I began to see my life's purpose differently. Intuitively I felt that my life in beautiful St. John, where I had lived for over two decades, was about to shift. The energy had changed. I had changed. When the house sold very quickly, I felt it was divine intervention. The message was clear. I was prepared and ready to risk it all. It was time to move and there was no turning back. I had no definitive plan but to completely trust in the divine unfolding.

Through my mantra meditation practice, I connected with my inner Self. As I continued to connect spiritually, my inner resources were also expanding. I trusted my intuition. I would run the decisions I was making by others for support. Even though Mom was not physically there to talk to, I asked my inner self to draw on those admirable qualities in her, the ones I relied on and valued. In doing so, I awakened to the fact that those aspects of her were also the qualities already inside of me. It's so true. We are like our mothers in many ways.

I was stepping into my authentic self. My way of being was growing and taking on a new shape. I was evolving. The pressure, stress and responsibilities I was experiencing during this time of great change led me to dig deeper into my inner resources. I was the full grown butterfly emerging from the cocoon, stretching into my freedom and ready to take flight.

Accessing and developing your inner resources and your personality traits is vital in coping with stress and moving through obstacles so you may heighten your true potential. It was through strengthening my resources that I emerged, more whole, from what would seemingly be seen as stressful overload, to living my life with calm centeredness.

I'm honored to be able to share with you six inner resources, six of my inner secrets for living through change, challenges and risk taking.

Unconditional Love

Love is the most important inner resource for me. Unconditional love is about loving another without a set of requirements or expecting to receive something in response your love. Aligning with love is the basis for which everything in life holds meaning. The true spiritual Self only knows love, so expressing love is communing with the divine. Receive love from others and from nature. Let yourself be nurtured and supported. Circulate the power of divine love. Live as a being of light and be the light for others.

I believe love and compassion go hand in hand. Compassion blossoms out of love and does not look for anything in return, not even an expression of gratitude. Living from a place of love and compassion allows you to be more understanding and accepting. You begin to see life through different lens. Reach out to aid those in need, even if that means your life may be put on hold or may change drastically. You may not be able to see the bigger picture at first. It is not necessary to fully understand the deeper meaning or purpose to be able to take action. It will all work out in the end; for everything is as it is, and in perfect order.

Silence

Silence is a powerful inner resource. One way of observing silence is by refraining from communicating through words or gestures and opening your awareness to the interconnectedness and unity of all that surrounds you. When I observe silence, I feel great solace and calmness. I love to sit in nature and feel my relationship to all living things. For me, silence alters perceptions and makes order out of chaos.

The practice of meditation is another way of being silent. It allows you tap into that silence between your thoughts for greater access to your true Self and liberation. Trying to figure out what to do next in the midst of a cluttered mind or coming from a place of ego is limiting. Aligning with your true Self, as opposed to your ego false self, helps you see possibilities without limitations. Sparks of inspiration, creative potentials and happiness are found in the silence.

Forgiveness

For most people this is the hardest concept to understand. Forgiveness is letting go of blame and not falling prey to victimization. I knew I needed to forgive certain individuals who cared for Mom in the hospital. The many unanswerable questions would dissolve into a place of forgiveness, but not until a year later. Forgiving is the way to love yourself so you can let go and move on. My power strengthened in the ability to relinquish the ego's need to be right and win. I let go of the anger by accepting that in life, mistakes are bound to me made, and by stepping into the shoes of the other players to know they did their best, without meaning any harm. Our beliefs and opinions are only one point of view from our limited perceptions of what we believe to be real.

Intuition

Every one of us has intuition. Whether or not we pay attention to it is another story. Intuition is a knowing, sensing and feeling about something before it happens. It's about listening to your heart or your gut, tapping into your internal wisdom. These messages are full of insight and knowledge. Your intuition lets you sense when things will be ideal, safe or supportive...or not. You don't know how you know, you just know you know.

When I need to make a decision, sometimes I close my eyes and ask myself the question that needs an answer. I listen to, or see what pops into my mind first before my conscious reasoning has a chance to cancel it out or negate it as nonsense. Once I feel it intuitively and decide to make a change, I do not let doubt enter. I trust and follow the choices, which I sense and soulfully feel to be true. The answers arise from a deeper level of consciousness that is not influenced by an ulterior motive of the ego.

Throughout my life, I have relied on my intuitive abilities. The little bird on my shoulder would be there if and when I was ready to listen without doubt. When I did listen and trust, all of the pieces and parts of my transition from St.

John to Florida fell into place smoothly. I sensed my intuitive perceptions and choices were spiritually aligned. There was a lighter feeling inside my body. My heart felt open. I was free to fly.

Taking Risks

Dive into the unknown. It's about courage and bravery. It can be exciting or scary. You can forge ahead or succumb to self-doubt. When was the last time you took a risk so you could fly? A big risk for me was leaving my life in St. John, saying goodbye to my friends, the island way of life and the work I had created there for 27 years. I am now taking a risk, once again, stepping authentically and fully into my higher purpose vision.

Recently, at the Women's Prosperity Network's Un-Conference, I had the opportunity to walk, barefoot, on broken glass. As I approached the glass, apprehension surfaced. The timing for this risk-taking activity was apropos. I trusted and took the risk. Afterwards, I felt exhilarated. A few days later, I had an epiphany. I was driving when I received a clear message. I whipped out my phone and began recording.

Here are the five things I learned from my experience of walking on glass...

1. Direction:

As you move forward don't turn back.
As you look forward don't look back.
Don't look down or veer off your path.
Be flexible.

2. Pace:
Don't walk too slowly or too fast, keep a steady pace.
Keep the momentum and energy flowing.
Don't hesitate or stop.
Take one step at a time, one foot in front of the other.
Be firm in your steps.
Walk consciously with relaxed awareness.

3. Be Present:
Breathe.
Stay focused and alert.
Don't be distracted.
Be aware of the steps you take.
Be mindful of what's happening around you.
Be aware of sudden changes.

4. Trust:
Believe in yourself.
Don't doubt.
Have faith.
Step outside your comfort zone.
Be at one with the experience.
Keep your vision in focus.

5. Support:
Gather friends around you to support you, cheer you on, raise you up and celebrate with you.
Acknowledge you did not do it alone.
Help others to succeed.
Be thankful when you reach a goal.

Gratitude

This last inner secret I will share here has the power to change the quality of your life, as well as your relationship with those around you. The multitude of gifts that surround us can be easily overlooked or taken for granted, especially in times of uncertainty, pain or suffering. These are the times gratitude can bring great happiness.

During my period of grief, I found one thing I was grateful for each day. I would take something I was grieving for and turn it around into something that I was grateful for. Here are three examples. I grieved I had witnessed Mom's pain. I was grateful I was with her, and I was grateful that she was not alone when she passed. I grieved that my mother had suffered greatly during her hospitalization and was grateful that her final hours were peaceful. I grieved the loss of my mother and was grateful to have had the perfect mother for me.

Give thanks daily to yourself, your divine Source and those who afforded you love and support along the way. Acknowledge your appreciation of all that nature has to offer. I invite you to delve deeper, spiritually and emotionally, to find the blessings upon which your life will flourish.

As my path continues to unfold, I am grateful for the gift of unconditional love and compassion I received from my mother, the opening of my heart to forgiveness, the gift of silence, trusting myself and a higher power to be able to take risks in life and to give thanks to all who have loved and supported me through this beautiful experience called life.

About the Author

Photo by Donna Marie Solensky

Jan Kinder is a leader in the field of holistic health and spiritual well being. For over three decades, she has been guiding individuals through the practice of meditation, holistic stress management, mind-body medicine and vibrational therapies. Clients say that she has changed their lives forever. As a speaker and workshop facilitator, Jan is considered a "highly skilled, warm hearted presenter with integrity and compassion." She is dedicated to inspire and help foster a more balanced, conscious society for the purpose of creating a positive change in the world.

Jan is a licensed, registered nurse; board certified holistic nurse, certified music therapist and credentialed Chopra Center Instructor. She founded The Jan Kinder Center for Health and Well Being in South Florida, formerly the award winning Self Centre International at the prestigious Caneel Bay Resort, St. John, USVI.

Connect with Jan at www.JanKinderCenter.com or Jan@JanKinderCenter.com

Vote for Hope!

Christine Gregory Campos

"There is only hope when you can still help."

This story is dedicated to Catherine for her bravery. The finality of death is unchangeable. There are no do-overs, no retakes, no second or third chances...it is done. It can be devastating for those left behind. Death is harsh, it does not answer back.

When faced with the death of a loved one, the space we have in our hearts for them aches in a way we rarely experience. The pain of losing a child is truly indescribable. I always thought I could truly feel the pain someone might have felt in this loss, but the reality of actually losing my first born son has taught me differently. The loss of a child leaves a gaping hole in your heart and soul, creates disharmony in your entire being and leaves death inside you.

On May 25, 2012, I received the horrific news that my son had overdosed and died. I felt an immediate pain in my womb, as if someone shot a hole right through me hitting my heart and my womb at the same time. This hollow pain still remains. The intensity changes from day to day, yet it does not leave. A mother should never have to lose their child. Sadly, so many parents and grandparents, brothers and sisters, aunts and uncles know the pain of losing a precious child in their family.

How did things go so wrong? What more could I have done? What was my part in this process of such profound loss? If it takes a village to raise a child, then it takes a village to lose one as well.

Two days after Brendon passed, I fought myself even to get out of bed each day and to continue on for the sake of my two other beautiful children, Brianna and Ryan. My entire being needed to "understand" and make sense of what and why I would be faced with such an experience.

Today, drugs are our children's # 1 killer. Addiction is a pandemic. Every 19 minutes someone dies from overdose. That is 72 people per day, 504 people per week, 2184 people per month, 26,208 people per year. Alarmingly, these numbers are on the rise since 2010.

It seems surreal, growing up in America, in the age where there is an ongoing *so called* war on drugs. My children went through the D.A.R.E. program, (Drug Abuse Resistance Education) as did every child in the public school system, yet today drugs are more prevalent and so easily accessible.

I live my life by the saying... *"I don't know what I don't know until I know I didn't know it."*

I turned to books, searching for answers and comfort immediately following my son's passing. I was aware of the Akashic Records, also known as the Book of Life. In these records, we documented our intentions and the lessons we wanted to learn for this lifetime. We created "soul contracts" with others in an effort to help each other learn the lessons we intended to learn. I needed so much to know and understand why I would have ever agreed to such a contract. Why would I have ever agreed to my son passing at the age of 23? Why would I submit myself to this type of incredible pain? It did not make sense to my human understanding.

In October, 2009, I was on Siesta Key Beach where I met Wendy, an Angel Intuitive. She said, "Christine, you are going to help heal addiction. You and Brendon have a soul contract." I remember thinking, "Really? How am I going to help heal addiction?" Looking back, I now see so much more than I did that day. That brings me to this conversation, a conversation that can make a difference.

When I heard of the opportunity to share a story in my life of a conversation that made a difference, I realized that sharing a conversation I didn't have with my son could potentially make the difference in hundreds, perhaps even thousands of lives. Even if this conversation only makes a difference in one single life, that one life touches so many other lives, and the energy of that one life can change our world.

The focus of this story is not to go in depth in our personal story. When Brendon passed on, I said to my family, "well the nightmare is over, and now the heartache begins".

The morning I got the call of Brendon's passing, I was online with my business mentors. They were so wonderful, caring and supportive. Thank you, Maria Gudelis, Tina Williams and **Trish Gilliam**. Over that weekend, they encouraged me take my pain and transform it in an effort to perhaps change the outcome for another soul on this planet. When I wrote my son's eulogy, these words came to me: "If there really is a war on drugs, where is the wall of the fallen? If addiction is a disease, where is the walk for our cure"?

My mentor's advice was truly a saving grace for me, as it has helped me to manage and "push through" my grief. Just as I had pushed through Brendon's birth, I had to push through his death. "The Brendon Project-A Project of Love" was launched November 25th, 2012, exactly six months to the day of Brendon's passing. As a professional marketing technologist, I used my skills to create the website and social sites as first steps in launching this cause.

The front page of the site is the "wall of the fallen". Each person lost to overdose has a story. There's a human being who is the "fallen". So many other humans, seemingly invisible, are behind the very visible death of this person, and are deeply affected by the devastating loss of their loved one. When you visit the wall and click into the picture of any person on the wall, you'll get that person's personal story.

By putting real faces and stories behind the word *addict,* demonstrating each loss, we *humanize* the soul behind the addiction and create a visual representation of the horrific loss of life, in the hope of creating a paradigm shift in how we perceive and treat addiction. I encourage people to add their loved one's story to the wall. Many people will not pay tribute to their loved one because of shame and guilt. Sadly, these emotions accompany the grief that comes with losing a loved one to addiction. This is a direct result of the outdated, antiquated messaging still existing around addiction today.

The second part of the project focuses on research development for better answers in addiction treatment. If addiction is a disease, where is the walk for our cure? I really *knew,* as mothers do, that I was unable to get Brendon the help he needed. I knew he was very *ill.* I knew that the programs and assistance available to him were failing him and ultimately failed his family, *my family.* I was so frantic and frightened when my son was alive, seemingly at a total loss of how I could help him. I also realized after he passed that if Brendon had had cancer, we would have rallied around him with every possible treatment available to bring him back to whole health. But we don't treat addiction that way. Instead, we were fighting legal battles, and it was never a topic I rushed to tell family and friends. I ask you to ponder the following question from your heart center:

"If we continue to treat addiction as a criminal matter, how can we ever truly treat it as a disease?"

I was working with Brendon using an "untraditional" approach, based on "whole love" not "tough love". I was raised to believe:

"Love is patient, love is kind. It does not envy, it does not boast, it is not proud. It does not dishonor others, it is not self-seeking, it is not easily angered, it keeps no record of wrongs. Love does not delight in evil but rejoices with the truth. It always protects, always trusts, always hopes, always perseveres. Love never fails. But where there are prophecies, they will cease; where there are tongues, they will be stilled; where there is knowledge, it will pass away."
1 Corinthians 13:4-8
New International
Version (NIV)

Brendon had been kicked out of rehab, another story for another book. I could not find any other program in which to place him, and since we drained the finances on legal matters, I was trying to treat him through what I learned. We were using a holistic medical approach to detox him.

Brendon made a huge improvement, but he needed much more than detox. Due to an open legal matter relative to his addiction, he had to return to New Jersey for a court date.

He left Tampa on a Tuesday, and by Friday he was dead. I had to do so many thing immediately following Brendon's passing. I had to make decisions I never thought I would ever have to make, decisions no mother should have to make. I had to take actions I never imagined I would take. I had to tell other people that I loved that my first born son had overdosed and died. It was all so surreal. I had to let his attorney know that Brendon was gone. Here is the email I wrote that day, along with his response:

On May 25, 2012, at 3:23 PM, "Christine - Gmail" wrote:

> Dear Brendon's Attorney:
> *Brendon returned home on Tuesday, as we had made prearrangements for travel so he could make the May 24 court date -not knowing it would change.*
> *Brendon died this morning of what we think was an overdose in NY City visiting his girlfriend.*
> *Christine Gregory Campos*
>
> *Christine-*
> *I am so sorry for you, Brendon and everyone else who loves him. I can't imagine the pain you're going through. I've defended hundreds of people in Brendon's position and none of them had such a loving and caring mother like you. Again, I'm sorry.*

I maintain: *If we continue to treat addiction as a criminal matter, how can we ever truly treat it as a disease?*

All the apologies in the world cannot change the finality of Brendon's death. Like most moms, I was insisting on complete 100% abstinence, an "all or nothing" approach. My belief system about addiction at the time was still pretty rooted in the "Just Say No" and "Anonymous" messages of the 1970's. I believe these outdated, narrow viewed messages play a huge role in today's death toll. What is really clear to me today is this:

Often times, there is a very long road between addiction, recovery and abstinence.

The road to complete abstinence is traveled by very few.

The lessons I've learned since my son's passing are the inspiration behind this conversation. The more I have read and learned, the more I have understood about addiction. My single intention is to share this information with the hope that perhaps it will touch and help the life of another.

The biggest lesson I have learned since Brendon's passing is that overdose from opiates is preventable! Yes, it is PREVENTABLE! Yet we continue to lose over 30,000 people a year to overdose.

FACT: Opiate overdose is reversible.

When a person overdoses on an opiate, like heroin or Oxycontin, the brain actually forgets to breathe. The narcotic invades the area of the brain function that manages breathing, and so the person just stops breathing.

FACT: There is and has been an antidote to reverse the process of overdose for over 50 years. Naloxone, also called by its trade name, "NARCAN", is a prescription drug that has been in use for over 50 years by EMT, Medical Professionals,

ERs and sometimes law enforcement to stop an overdose in its process.

If the drug is administered in a timely manner, it can actually reverse the overdose as it happens. NARCAN (or naloxone), when administered, works immediately! It goes right to the brain and boots the narcotic out of the area of the brain that manages the function of breathing. In my mind, it can be compared to an Epi-Pen, in that if someone was having a severe allergic reaction the lack of access to an Epi-pen could be fatal. If we realize someone is *"at risk"* for overdose, why are we not giving these people the same level of medical care options we would for any other disease, be it physical or mental?

I found a bottle of naloxone in Brendon's room when going through his items. Why didn't I know about this life saving information when Brendon was alive? How could such a critical measure to prevent or reverse overdose not be a well publicized matter, especially in the wake of our current pandemic of addiction?

One very true, sad fact is this: *The addict most at risk for overdose is one who is new to recovery or leaving a rehab program.* I read a story by a mom who said, "I wish now that I had not focused solely on abstinence for my son, but that I would have thought to give him "survival" skills for the "road of recovery." God, how I wish the same.

I am thankful for those who have been placed in my path since the loss of my son. Denise and Gary Cullen have been instrumental in connecting me to others who are on this path to *"heal addiction."* Denise is the Executive Director and Gary is the Vice President and CFO of both GRASP – "Grief Recovery After Substance Passing", and "Broken No More."

They lost their only son Jeff to overdose in 2008. I am not alone in this mission. There are many working toward harm reduction, changing laws and funding medical research on drug use and addiction. Denise invited me to attend the October, 2013 Drug Policy Alliance (DPA) Conference held in Denver.

At the conference, I was graced to meet Eliza Wheeler, from Harm Reduction Coalition. She is the DOPE Project Manager (Drug Overdose and Prevention Education). As I listened to her speak at the conference, I learned more about naloxone, this life saving drug and the information on how to use it. Eliza also performed a demonstration of administering naloxone for the moms who were there from different organizations. She also provided me time on the phone, post conference to interview her further so I could be sure to share accurate and helpful information.

I really took this information to heart. Naloxone gives mothers another chance to save the lives of their addicted children. I set up a resource page for you to get the "facts" about naloxone, including a link to my full interview with Eliza, where I asked very important questions pertaining to naloxone. These facts include the drug's safety use, which types of drug overdoses naloxone can reverse, as well as the laws that impact naloxone distribution and availability.

There are also additional links which Eliza provided that are useful for finding resources in your local area.

While I started the Brendon Project hoping it would be a catalyst of change, in the end the *organizations* are not the heart of the matter. It is this message of hope – of *life* that matters. It is very simple. One Voice, One Love. I realized that the most important action I could take was to share the message of hope – the hope that lies in naloxone.

In closing this conversation, I encourage you to not get lost in discouragement over this incredibly crippling matter of addiction. The most important message is 'yes, we can save a life'.

Safe and alive is another chance for the next *breath* of hope. It allows for that do over, that second chance –it allows for something which death does not – *life*. So my vote is for hope. Will you stand with me and *VOTE* for Hope? Claim your "Victory Over Today's Epidemic."

"When something goes wrong, we all get together, because together we are strong".
~Brendon Michael Campos (3/7/89 – 5/25/12)

Resources

Visit www.preventoverdose.com and that will bring you to a page on The Brendon Project containing all the resources and organizations mentioned in this chapter.

A heart full of thanks to Tony Khoury for his never ending support. So many thanks to Jerry McCoy from New WordPress Plugin, for volunteering as senior technical advisor. A special thanks to Dr. Scott Styles who was instantly there for me, spending hours coaching me gently through grief. Thanks to Neil (a.k.a. Kitch) Ward for never giving up hope on our efforts for The Brendon Project. Thanks to Elaine Lindsay for helping with The Brendon Project graphics. Heartfelt thanks to Denise and Gary Cullen, GRASP and Broken No More for taking me under their wings on this path of working to healing addiction. Thanks to Barry

Lessin from Broken No More for sharing his insights to working with addiction. HUGE thanks and big hugs to Eliza Wheeler of Harm Reduction Coalition, for the time she spent educating me on naloxone. Thanks to Moms United, a campaign of A New PATH (Parents for Addiction Treatment & Healing) for taking me in as part of their group at the Drug Policy Alliance Conference. Thanks to Drug Policy Alliance and all these organizations, as they have been instrumental in my learning this message. *Godspeed to all those involved in "healing addiction".*

I encourage you to get involved and share your voice on the matters concerning addiction, treatment and the drug war. Visit the Drug Policy Alliance and find out more about addiction, harm reduction and the drug war. You won't believe what you don't know.

"Question Everything –Think For Yourself!"
~Brendon Michael Campos (3/7/89 – 5/25/12)

About the Author

Christine Gregory Campos, Intuitive Business Marketing Strategist with Marketing Intentionally, lives in Tampa, Florida with her son Ryan. Her daughter Brianna, now 23, has returned to college for her Masters Degree in Counseling. Christine is the Founder and Creator of The Brendon Project, a Project of Love. She has joined the energy of many other organizations working to change the "face" of addiction and find better answers to addiction treatment.

To find out more about Christine visit
www.about.me/ChristineGregoryCampos

For more information about the Brendon Project and Vote for Hope, please go to

http://www.thebrendonproject.com/

Christine's email addresses:

christine@thebrendonproject.com

christine@marketingintentionally.com

Hidden Secrets to Honest Talk

Gayle D'Haeseleer

As I sat through the movie where Dame Judy Dench plays a woman who was brutally separated from her young son while in a nunnery for unwed mothers, I carefully digested the unfolding of events. In relation to her life, the compassion and her ability to extend forgiveness to her perpetrators, despite what she had been through, I couldn't help but correlate the happenings in the life of Philomena to my own mother.

I flew in to Chicago in 1984, with my then husband (my "wasbund"), to enjoy Thanksgiving with my family in Lake Forest at my brother's home. He was hosting the holiday. After having had a few prosperous years, he had decided to fly the entire family to his home on his dime. Beautiful!

While dodging the occasional drama at the family holiday gathering, the ever present alcohol and "doobee" and the rest of the festive partying, I was doing my best to keep it all together with an infant, a 2 year old and a completely vacant spouse.

I had suspected, for a long time before this event, that my mother's life was a little less than harmonic as a child. Come to think about it, it was quite obvious, actually, since she had always been secretive about her family and her past. In fact, she was downright unresponsive when I asked her about her life, her parents and my grandparents. She would always aptly avoid the subject and as I got older it became less easy for her not to answer my questions. I sensed that there was an extensive amount of fear behind her unwillingness to talk about her past.

So, naturally, I was curious about my mother's family. I wanted to know who these people were. Did I resemble them? What they were like? Who were they? I wanted to know. Who would send a young girl away with so many unanswered questions and why? I knew that I would never hold judgment so rigid as to alienate a child I had created and so loved because of a past mistake. Who could be so cold?

She kept us away from her family. She had told me that she was Scotch-Irish, her mother was Irish and her Father was Scottish. As I got older, I pressed on to know their names. When I got to my grandfather's name, she said, "Stanley." I would incredulously and unceremoniously chortle, "Stanley?" Are you sure we aren't Polish? What self respecting Irish/Scottish woman would name their kid Stanley?!! Something wasn't copasetic in Denmark. She had left a few clues in the past. She did say, when pressed, that she had issues with her family as a youngster and that she had been in a Catholic boarding school. She claimed to have been dropped off there and had limited contact with her family from then on. Feeling like something had to be very wrong for a 12 year old young girl to be separated from her family, never to have any meaningful contact again, sent my wonderment and bewilderment into overtime in my imagination.

As I think back, even putting myself in my mother's shoes, I realize that nothing could have motivated me to take the path and guard the castle to the degree that my mother did. I also have compassion for my mother and what she had to endure. She closed up as a way to protect herself and maybe the child.

Contrarily, I really loved listening to the stories my father told us of his side of the family. He was very proud of the fact that we had evolved from a pioneer family arriving in the New Colonies from England at Plymouth Rock. He would occasionally take us to the cemetery where some of our ancestors were buried, including his mother and father, step-parents, siblings, cousins and additional family members. I even saw the homestead where he and his 6 brothers and sister were raised. We were also privy to information of the indiscretions of the infamous members of the family. I still go there to investigate, exploring the evolution of the family and the area.

On one of the nights around the massive fireplace, while in Chicago for Thanksgiving, enjoying an evening aperitif with my brothers and sisters, having all of our children tucked in nicely, a question arose. It instigated a slow interrogation of my father that set my brain afire. I learned that trying to acquire Social Security for my mother was something of a challenge. Apparently, they could not find her name in the Social Security files or the census records. Her children had to each present their birth certificates. Those documents lead to additional birth for a child that was born before my eldest brother and sister. A baby! One before all of us? I was stunned. Somewhere out there, I might have a half brother or sister! I knew it! I knew it was something having to do with the Catholic Church and that boarding school she talked about. It had been alluded to that the church didn't like the fact that my father was not "of the faith." I knew it was something bigger. But what was it?

My father had said that it was some kind of a "back seat affair" that had caused her to become pregnant out of wedlock, ultimately causing that part of her life to become a huge secret. In my process of thinking through this, looking for answers myself, I recalled my mother being extremely judgmental of her own children as they began to explore sex and their own sexuality in their young adult lives.

Dad swore us to secrecy, as he had promised my mother to keep her personal business to themselves and not divulge something that she had carried so much shame about. He also felt we should know. Not everything, but maybe just this little piece of the puzzle.

In the midst of it all, a baby shows up in her half sister's house, but since I was never able to know her family, it might be impossible to know the truth. Why? Because no one was ever allowed to talk about sex, or educated about what to do when the pressure to participate presented itself. No one was ever allowed to talk about it. The joys or the consequences of this natural part of life were consistently swept under the proverbial rug, leaving women of the day to face the "consequences" of their ignorance about their natural desires.

After the interrogation of my father, I never talked about it again. I respected my parent's wishes for privacy. I carried around that knowledge in a little compartment in my head, knowing that, someday, I might be able to approach the subject again. After my father died in 1991, I was alone with Mom in her living room. I knew this could be the moment. I reminded her of the great Thanksgiving weekend and relived the story with her. She looked at me with a straight gaze into my eyes and said it was a long time ago and that at the time, she did what she thought was best for us.

My mother had changed her name. That's why no one could contact her. She didn't want to be found. I believe she had to be reconciled to that part of her life from so long ago before she could allow anyone to know anything. I wanted to know, and she knew I wanted to know, but she was incapable of sharing this secret that had created such guilt and shame in her life. My heart breaks to think of what my mother and other women went through at that time in their lives.

Throughout history, we have learned that when women were unwed and pregnant, they were shut away in convents and homes for unwed mothers for the sake of not disgracing their families in a time that society found this to be so totally unacceptable. Who knows what really happened in those cloistered environments. No one really knows whether the girls were worked harshly during their time there, or if at the time of the birth they were ever even allowed to see the child. More often than not, the baby was whisked away to the adoption agency that would then find a suitable family home in which to place the child.

I've learned, throughout my lifetime, that forgiveness is the key. It the key to living a free and beautifully full life. Philomena is an incredible example of how you can forgive and still search for that which is missing. She, and my mother, both lived their lives the way that was best for each of them. And I have to do my part in forgiving Mom for not sharing that we were only living a short distance from my half sibling and all of my extended family. I forgive my mother for doing that, and at the same time, like Philomena, it won't stop me from looking for them.

Through this all, I wanted to create, and have created, an atmosphere of open communication and honest conversation with my own children about human sexuality. I knew that this type of honest conversation about the birds and the bees could ultimately help them to avoid making choices, or being in situations that would create unwanted results

This entire conversation, both about my mother's circumstance and my desire to have a different environment in my own home, has set me on a mission. I want to offer families and students the opportunity to learn how to have the same kind of open, honest conversation that I have had in my home with my own children as a result of all that is in my mother's past and the emotions her circumstances had created in my own life. Education is one thing. Talking about what you learn in a safe, loving environment is another. Supporting our young adult children through their natural explorations is one of the ways that we can intervene on behalf of the families that may be affected as a result of youthful ignorance. Even today, when sex is an open conversation in the world, it is still a closed one in most of our homes. It is in the home, that personal space, where we can have the conversation that will make a difference in the lives our own children and grandchildren.

I challenge you to open your minds and your hearts to this level of communication in your homes and in our schools so that we, as a society, in this generation can be spared victimization, guilt, shame, disgrace, and loss of family.

About the Author

Gayle D'Haeseleer is an entrepreneur who believes that honest communication in business and family is key to building great relationships and avoiding potentially disastrous situations. As the married mother of six, Gayle has learned to juggle family and finance throughout the years. Gayle says that she, herself is her only challenge. Be courageous, be allowing, be accepting, let go, find forgiveness and just love.

Connect with Gayle at gayledhaeseleer@gmail.com

From Little Thievery to Powerful Parenting

Pat Douglas

I was raised by my paternal grandparents in Washington, D.C. My parents separated when I was three years old. I didn't remember my mother as I was growing up, and the majority of my happy memories of my father were few and far between. My mother remarried and settled in another state and never contacted me. My paternal grandmother felt it was important that I, at least, know my daddy even if my association with him was in a totally negative environment. Thus, my earliest memories of my daddy were occasional visits on a Sunday morning to Lorton Penitentiary in Virginia. I knew my daddy was in prison because he had stolen money that didn't belong to him.

The prison had many red brick buildings enclosed with high chain link fences with barbed wire at the top. On Sunday mornings there were long lines of visitors waiting to be cleared before being allowed entrance to the huge room to wait for the prisoners. When my daddy entered the room, I was all smiles. I would sit on his lap while he talked to Grandma and my Aunt Doris, daddy's younger sister. These are my earliest memories of my daddy. I never remember him being there on Christmas, Easter, or my birthday. All of my early memories of him are a crowded room in a prison. On each visit, he promised me that one day he would come home and things would be different.

Many years later after I married, I decided to take my four year old daughter, Eve, to purchase some new dresses at Woodward and Lothrop Department Store in Annapolis, Maryland, where we lived. I selected three adorable dresses and while the sales clerk was ringing up the sale, I noticed that Eve was happily checking out the display of Snoopy items. Since the store was only five miles from our house, I knew I would have ample time to return home and prepare dinner. I had no idea of the impact of that late afternoon excursion.

When we arrived home from the department store, Eve went to her bedroom to play, and I started preparing dinner. Once dinner was in the oven and the table was set, I went to Eve's room to check on her.

"Hi honey, what are you coloring?" I asked.

"Hi Mommy, I'm making a pretty picture with my Snoopy pencils!" she responded.

I glanced at the small packet on the floor and instantly recognized the Snoopy colored pencils. I then asked, "Eve, where did you get those?" In an instant, I knew I had to make the right decision.

My darling four year old looked up and answered, "I brought them home from the store."

"Oh honey, we didn't pay for those. You can't take something from the store; you have to pay money for them! We have to go back now. Put them back in the case."

Many years had passed since that day, but I still remember it vividly. A couple of years ago I received a telephone call from my daughter who is now married and has a family. She told me she and her husband, Dennis, went to a sporting goods store to purchase sneakers for their two boys, 11 year old Sean and 9 year old Jack. The boys tried on several different brands and styles and eventually selected the ones they both wanted.

"Mom and Dad, thanks for the new shoes! Where are we going to dinner?" Sean inquired as they left the store.

"We're going to a restaurant close by since this is a school night." responded their dad.

Once they had submitted their drink order, the boys proceeded to take small toys out of their pockets to play with them.

Eve immediately asked, "Where did you get those?"

Sean answered, "Out of the shoe boxes. No one else wanted them!"

Eve responded, "You were only supposed to receive the toy from the box you purchased, not the toys in all the other boxes!" She grabbed her purse and said, "Let's go, Dennis, we need to take these back to the store."

Dennis asked, "Can't we do this after we eat?"

"No, absolutely not! We need to go now!" She exclaimed.

When they returned to the sporting goods store, she asked to speak with the manager. Dennis asked her, "Why can't we simply talk to the girl who waited on us?"

Eve felt the girl who waited on them was probably 18, or younger, and she didn't want her to let the boys off easily. "No, we need to speak with the manager." She affirmed.

When the manager arrived, Eve explained that her boys were there to apologize and return items that they had stolen. The manager totally understood and said, "You know, I could call the police now to come here, and they could take you to the police station!" By this time, the younger one's lip was quivering and the older one's eyes were focused on the floor. After a good talking to by the manager, Sean looked up and said, "I'm sorry!" Then Jack looked up with a tear in his eye and said, "I'm sorry, too!" The manager then explained to them the gravity of their theft and all the consequences. She also told them she would not call the police because they had returned the items. By the time the family left the store, both boys were scared and apologetic.

Once dinner was completed and the boys were home in bed, Dennis asked Eve, "Why did you insist on doing that right away, and why did you want to speak to the manager?"

Eve then explained to him that at the age of four, her mom returned her to the department store because she had taken some small colored pencils from a Snoopy display. She said the older lady in the department store told her she had stolen them. She said it was against the law, and she could go to jail. It made a lasting impression on her for the rest of her life. She said she knew the young clerk would probably say, "Oh, its okay, thanks for returning them." Eve expected the manager to say what the boys needed to hear.

After my daughter told me about the boys, she mentioned that when she went shopping with girl friends as a teenager, she witnessed some of them stealing. She remembered that lesson and made sure she left the store so she would not be associated with them. She always remembered that one moment of being confronted and humiliated by the manager and what the consequences were.

Many times people overlook or brush things under the rug instead of using that moment to teach a valuable lesson. The extra effort that it took to return a four year old girl to the department store, or two boys to the sporting goods store, was well worth the time because a valuable lesson can be experienced from the conversation that takes place.

I learned a valuable lesson by visiting my daddy in prison. My grandmother always told me he committed a crime, and he was paying the price for it by spending years in prison. I realized as a small child that I never wanted my life to turn out that way. My daddy spent six years in that prison and another five years in a federal prison in Atlanta. This was an extremely negative part of my childhood. I passed my experience and lesson along to my daughter, and my daughter has passed it on to her sons. It only takes one moment in each of our lives to make a difference in someone else's life.

The words said by a manager in a store were impactful because they were coming from someone other than the parent. Our words as parents, relatives, friends or strangers can be important. It can be a simple, "Hello, how are you today?" to a stranger in the grocery store. The person you are speaking to may be a lonely senior citizen. That simple "Hello..." with a smile on your face may be the only person that has taken time to greet them all week.

We can all make a difference in others' lives if we remember that what we say *does* matter. What we say may be e*xactly* what someone else needs to hear.

"The art in conversation lies in listening."
~Malcolm Forbes

About the Author:

Pat Douglas was born and raised in Washington, D.C. At the age of nineteen she moved to New Jersey and worked for the National Board of the YWCA. When she returned to the Washington area, she went to work for the General Services Administration and Air Cargo, Inc. At the age of 25 she went to Europe alone and traveled throughout seven countries. This was the beginning of her love of travel. She has returned to Europe several times and has visited other countries, many islands and numerous states. Pat is a graduate of the University of South Florida with a B.A. Degree in Psychology and currently lives in the suburbs of Tampa, Florida. In addition to travel, she enjoys sewing, golf, sailing, and most of all - her three awesome grandsons. Her goal in life is to make a positive impact on others' lives. Pat is now an Independent Associate with LegalShield[SM], a 40 year old company that offers legal services and identity theft resolution and restoration at a very affordable cost.

Visit her website, http://www.PatDouglas.net for a complete description of plan benefits.

Change Your Story, Change Your Life

Janice Karm

Who do you spend most of your time communicating with? Whose voice do you recognize as the one you hear most often? Who has the most influence on how you show up in the world each and every day?

You may have guessed it. It's you!

Jack Canfield, co-creator of the "Chicken Soup for the Soul" book series, cites research indicating the average person thinks as many as 50,000 thoughts a day. That's right, we engage in self-talk thousands of times each day.

The conversations which make the most difference, those which have the most influence on our present day reality and our upcoming future, are those we have with ourselves. The majority of us do most of our communicating between our very own ears; we are our constant companion. Some of the most powerful messages we listen to are never heard by anyone other than ourselves. In fact, some are so insidious and sub-conscious that we often don't recognize them at a cognitive level. Yet, they significantly affect the actions we take and results we generate.

The words we choose, those unspoken and said aloud, impact the outcomes we manifest. It's important for us to become familiar with our inner voice, pay attention to what it says and the tone being used.

Research shows that individuals have two negative thoughts for every one positive thought. We have the ability to be our own best advocate or worst critic. The things we tell ourselves and the choices we make shape our reality.

Much of the dialogue we engage in stems from core beliefs, those things we learned as children and accepted as fact. Our parents and other significant individuals inadvertently passed on their own beliefs and we integrated many of them into our being. We didn't know to challenge what we heard; the internalized messages became our truth. This and our interpretations of feedback we received gave birth to our own belief system.

As we mature, become more insightful and continue gaining feedback, we are able to differentiate what truly resonates with us and what does not. We can step back and evaluate the self-talk and beliefs we've presumed up until then. We are able to filter out stories which no longer serve us and replace them, using the reasoning of an adult mind. We can contemplate whether our collective beliefs support or hinder us from living happily and fulfilled and if they move us towards or away from our purpose. We can choose to challenge and replace outdated beliefs with others more aligned with who we are today.

So, how do you do this?

To begin with, you must first create an awareness of your inner dialogue. One method for practicing this is by taking the role of an observer (of your thoughts) and listening without judgment. Listen with the perspective of "Isn't that interesting?" Let go of being the critic, just notice your thoughts.

What frame of reference do you see things through?

Simply drawing a different frame around the same set of circumstances brings new pathways into view.

What words do you use?

Does your vocabulary revolve around interpreting things as "good" or "bad", "better" or "worse", "right" or "wrong?" How often do you tell yourself you "should" or "must" do something? Do you find yourself saying "I can't"? Seek ways to alter your language.

Do you speak differently to yourself than others?

Are you more patient with others, less demanding or kinder? Do you show yourself the same respect and concern? Instead of lecturing or scolding yourself, talk to yourself as if you were talking to a child you love. Use words of encouragement, be gentle, and remember to forgive yourself.

Do you compare yourself to others?

Are you caught up in assessing yourself as someone "better than" or "worse than" another? Cease comparing and judging both yourself and others.

Are you truly present for what's going on around you?

Pay attention. How often are you listening to someone while thinking of something else, or involved in an activity while focusing on something like your grocery list? Make a deliberate attempt to be present.

Are you trying to achieve perfection?

What standards are you holding for yourself? Do you quit if it's "not good enough"? Remember, anything worth doing well is worth doing poorly at first.

Are you living authentically?

Do your thoughts and actions align with your values, beliefs and purpose? If not, how do you create congruency between what you say and what you do?

Do you think in terms of abundance or deficit?

Your mindset influences what you notice. If you view things as abundant, they become abundant.

Do you make a practice of recognizing all you have to be grateful for?

Whether it's a written list or spoken, this one tool can shift you from a negative to a positive frame in minutes. Make an exhaustive list and reflect on it.

Do you visualize your (positive) intended outcomes?

Becoming a Life Change Artist, by F. Mendell, Ph.D. and K. Jordan Ph.D. states the following on visualization, "It's proven to be very valuable to have a vision for your future life. Research shows that we are more likely to accomplish our goals when we picture them and clearly write them down."

Choose a day when you will record what you hear each time you recognize the self-talk. Make a conscious effort to catch yourself and write down what's coming up, no matter what it is. Notice the voice and tone. Whose is it? Is it a nurturing adult? Is it a task-master? What about a rebellious child? Does it seek to please others? Is it loud or does it whisper? Does it change based on circumstances and your overall disposition at the moment?

Engaging the services of a professional coach or therapist is greatly beneficial in both recognizing and interpreting deep-seated beliefs. A trained professional can help penetrate what's beneath the surface and assist in deciphering the myriad of thoughts rummaging through your mind. Many beliefs have been hanging around, haunting your subconscious since childhood. Attempt to understand the purpose they serve today. Were the (old) beliefs useful in the past, but managing to keep you stuck now? Strive to identify whether they continue to benefit you or just get in your way. Only then can you determine whether to hold on to them, let them go and/or replace them.

For instance, your inner voice, which is built upon core beliefs, might express that you are not working quickly enough and jeopardizing your agreed upon deadline. By recognizing the chatter, you can respond in several ways. It might sound like, "I'm working at a very good pace and feel confident in the work I'm doing." The cynical voice might counter with, "You won't be able to do this!" to which you can reply, "Really?" How do you know that? Is there any factual evidence to support your opinion? I haven't missed a deadline up until now" or alternatively, "Thanks for sharing, but I've got this covered. There's no need for you to hang around!" This will promote the effect of silencing the distrustful voice and allow you to continue working.

Whether you choose to take it further, at that moment or later, the awareness of self-talk provides an opportunity to reflect upon the message itself. Consider the purpose it serves. Are you using the voice to place pressure on yourself? Is that how you've learned to accomplish things? Do you think you'll fail if someone's not cracking the whip? Consider changing your frame and ask, "What about approaching this differently in the future? What would it be like to trust myself instead, knowing I'm accountable for the commitments I make?"

What follows are three real-life examples of my self-talk. In the first two, I lacked awareness that my inner dialogue was undermining my personal growth. In both of these, self-limiting beliefs drove my decisions and significantly altered the direction of my life. The third represents quite the opposite.

Changing My Story:
College, Freshman Year

As a first year art student, I excelled in graphic arts and enjoyed the creative force that flowed through me. Second semester, I registered for my first drawing class. We began with an assignment to sketch a paper bag (which the instructor had folded and then unfolded in many places). It was a study in light, dark and shadows. Unlike my classmates' finished drawings, mine looked nothing like the bag. Once completed, I looked at my project with disdain. I remember thinking it resembled the eruption of Mt. St. Helens (which coincidently, had done just that in the early 80s and was often in the news).

My inner voice insisted I could not draw and therefore I would not become an artist. Fear set in and I began searching for another major; one that was easy to excel in. As an eighteen year old with limited experience, I couldn't see past my self-limitations. Even as my guidance counselor tried reasoning with me, I was unable to even consider remaining in the program. In hindsight, I could have been a stellar

147

graphic artist BUT my definition of an artist didn't provide any room for negotiation. I KNEW I couldn't be an artist (the type of artist I had envisioned) so I wasn't going to become one!

Changing My Story:
From Social Worker to IT Professional

After several years as a social worker, I began searching for employment in the private sector. Not knowing which direction to take, I took on several temporary positions, hoping I'd find a good fit. One such position was as the Executive Secretary to the Director of IT. I was a quick touch-typist and good organizer; both being requirements for the job.

I had the finest electric typewriter (I was oh-so-grateful it wasn't manual), the IBM Selectric®. It was later replaced with a DisplayWriter® (an electronic stand-alone word processor). If it had been up to me, I would have kept the typewriter. I didn't see the need for the advanced technology.

My manager, Tony sought to replace the DisplayWriter® with a personal computer (after all, I was in IT and PCs were being mainstreamed in the office). My reply (again, based on my story and view of myself) was, "I'm a people person and I'm creative; I'm not meant to use computers."

After revising the departmental organization chart by hand, more than once, using Wite-Out® for edits, Tony decided it was time for me to use the department's PC. He handed me a manual and disk and directed me to create an electronic orgchart. I was frightened (self-talk: "I'm not going to be able to do this"). Somehow, I had convinced myself that only a certain type of person used computers and I was not one of them.

My internal dialogue and beliefs were inflexible. But, having been ordered to do so, I sat myself down at the PC and followed the step-by-step instructions. When I saw the output, I was delighted. The mere fact I had produced a printed representation of our department brought about a riveting change of mindset.

That evening I put a note on Tony's desk, asking for a PC of my own. I began teaching myself DOS (an operating system that some pre-Windows® and pre-Mac® users might remember). I took home a "portable" laptop (the size of a roll-aboard suitcase) and began educating myself on popular software programs.

Each morning, I came to the office energized with knowledge from the previous night. I arrived prepared with a list of questions and was tutored by both Tony and the System Administrator. I remember the excitement pulsing through me during that period. My world absolutely shifted. For the very first time, I recall thinking, "I'm smart." It had never occurred to me before. Remember, I was the nice and creative one. That was it. End of story.

I began seeing myself differently and redefining what I was capable of. I went on to have positions as a Trainer, Network Administrator, System Administrator, Customer Support Specialist, Business Developer and Program Manager, all within IT over a 24 year period.

These two brief examples demonstrate my ability to create a reality fitting my self-limiting beliefs. I talked myself out of becoming an artist and instead became a social worker. I almost kept myself from a fruitful career in IT. I was basing decisions on misinformation – the things I told myself that were not true.

Changing My Story:
Trusting in Myself and Following my Passion

I was employed by a major IT corporation for 15 years. The first 12 were awesome. I had opportunities to learn, grow and add value in ways I hadn't imagined. After having worked for many companies prior to this, I envisioned staying with the company until retirement.

Somewhere around my 12th year, I discovered I was no longer enjoying my work. As time went on, I felt less satisfied with my responsibilities and the direction of management. My spark faded. I felt as if the life had been sucked out of me. I invented a number of reasons to support being discontent, until I took responsibility for how I was creating and willingly participating in my own misery. Something needed to change.

I realized what I didn't want, yet had no idea what I did want. I was committed to discovering where I'd go next. I found myself in all types of situations wondering, "Could I see myself doing that?" I looked at internal and external job postings and asked, "Is this something I'd like to do?" I took online surveys and used career planning tools. I spoke with other people about what they were doing for a living. All the while, my inner dialogue said, "I trust I'll find what I'm looking for."

All of a sudden I became aware of the serendipity occurring around me. I witnessed miraculous events taking place in concert with each other. I read a book that moved me beyond words; it rekindled my desire to be in service to others. I emailed the two authors and we began corresponding. One suggested I look into becoming a coach. Having never been exposed to coaching, I researched the field, what type of training it entailed and employment opportunities.

Next I searched and signed up for a workshop geared towards self-discovery. I committed to take myself on – to understand where I was stuck and what I could do to transform my life. Only after having registering did I discover that both authors would be staffing the workshop (mere coincidence you ask?). Three weeks later, I walked into the workshop and witnessed people who were either employed or volunteering for the event. I became keenly aware of the workshop facilitator and his presence.

And then it happened. I knew right then and there. I wanted to work with people devoted to self-improvement and personal development. I wanted to facilitate others who were interested in defining and committing to their own excellence and the greatness of others. I decided to pursue certification as a Transformational Coach. I enrolled and became a student while still working full-time.

I had lost interest in being a corporate woman - it was over. I wanted to invest in what made me feel alive, passionate, useful and overall happy with who I was. I set aside a year's worth of funds to live on (during what I imagined would be a transition period) and requested to be laid off.

Can you imagine? In the midst of an economic crisis, with a well-paying position and great benefits, I took a leap of faith. I gained no support from my family, co-workers or friends. They were tapping into their own beliefs and I was unwilling to take them on as my own What I heard was, "You have a great job and income." "You are a single mom; you need to support yourself and your son." "How will you pay for college?" and "How will you do that without a job?" I refused to let fear compromise the intentions I held for myself. I continued to trust in the opportunities that would open up once I let go of what was no longer bringing me joy.

I found a way to unleash myself, discover my purpose and live my life with the passion that had been missing. I acted in accordance with my desires, not hastily, but with a carefully thought out action plan. I had faith and trust that the universe would support me. I received my coaching certification and started my own business, all in alignment with what I had discovered and made a choice to pursue.

As for you, what stories have you made up and bought into? Where are they holding you back? What might happen if you start communicating with yourself differently? What possibilities might open up if you change your story?

The very reason I chose coaching is to inspire others to embrace change, step into their possibilities and transform their lives. It's all about becoming acutely aware of what we want (and don't want), making choices to support our intentions and taking decisive action to attain our desired results. I call this The Possibility Formula...

Vivid Awareness + Abundant Choice + Inspired Action = Desired Results.

I invite you to go through an exercise of noticing your inner dialogue. Keep these points in mind:

- Consider your frame of reference
- Be conscious of the words you choose and your tone

- Speak nicely to yourself
- Resist comparing yourself to others and coming from a place of judgment
- Remain present
- Challenge the desire for perfection
- Be authentic
- View your world as abundant
- Practice gratitude
- Use the tool of visualization to create your own masterpiece, and then make it happen

I encourage you to seek other resources on the topics of core beliefs, frame of reference and self-talk. If you desire something more, better or different and you want additional joy, bigger results and greater personal success, consider changing your story – and changing your life.

About the Author

Janice Karm, commonly known as *Ms. Possibilities*, is the owner and Chief Possibility Officer of Possibilities Unlimited, LLC. She inspires others to embrace change, step into their possibilities and transform their lives. Janice encourages those who want more, better or different to recognize and take action on the endless opportunities awaiting them with her unique energy and insight. After 28 years of success in the corporate arena, Janice changed her professional direction to follow her true passion. She is a Certified Transformational Coach, public speaker, trainer, facilitator and author. Janice holds the belief that we can invite true happiness and joy into our lives when we become clear about what we want.

To find out more about exploring your possibilities, visit www.PossibilitiesUnlimited.com You can also email Ms. Possibilities at Janice@PossibilitiesUnlimited.com

Tears of a Clown

Paul Gruber

Out of the shadows, a rough hand powerfully grabbed my arm as I stepped off the curb. The burly crackling voice garbled, "Ey 'scuse me brotha.. but.. kin ya help me out?"

I turned to the 50 year old, dark skinned, weather worn face and quickly accessed the man. I assumed he was homeless and probably not too bright. The odor emitting from this man suggested he had been drinking and might be capable of anything. His grip loosened, for the moment I could stay, or I could go. I decided to stay.

His drunkenness made communication difficult, and his slurred street slang made communication almost comical. He pulled something out of his pocket. Whatever it was, he really wanted me to see it. In the darkness, I was only partially paying attention, as I was already, planning my exit strategy. I had a pretty good idea that he wanted, money, and I was not about to give money to a drunk.

I often have chats with homeless people. I had actually considered myself misunderstood growing up, and it angered me that people were forced to feel like outcasts. The thing was, when I had these chats, I was usually playing a role, feigning interest in others, hoping that one day I might genuinely care. That day was upon me, and I didn't even know it. As usual, tonight, I was busy thinking about myself, how unfair the world was and what was next on that night's journey through the city.

He violently gestured to the item he had pulled from his pocket while barking at me, saying something incomprehensible. My wandering mind snapped back to the present. I realized that I had to give this man my attention, but what did he want? The item he pulled from his coat was a wallet, and he insisted that I inspect his ID. Why did he want to identify himself? Leaning to one side almost to the point of toppling over, and then quickly snapping back up to attention, he sputtered, "Name's Kirkman. Staff Sergeant Mark Kirkman, served tweny twoo..." he nodded forward and then continued talking, "years in the armed forces." From what he was slurring out, I was able to piece together some story about running out of gas and needing to get back home. Apparently he lived about 35 minutes away so "fo fitty ($4.50) would do the trick."

He was a War Veteran just trying to get home. I told him, "Here's the situation man, I have no cash. If I did I would try to help you out, I really would. Are you hungry?" In truth, I had a few dollars that I did not want to give to him, especially if he really did have a Camaro sitting nearby, because that man behind the wheel would have been bad news. Almost as if he did not hear me, the man began listing the items he was willing to trade for money, starting with a Seiko watch. The items got progressively less appealing; a shoestring, a handful of paperclips, until he offered me a ring from the war containing different colored stones that created a rising or setting sun. On the side of the ring were eagles and two little figures. He explained to me that he planned to keep the ring forever, it meant the world to him, yet he really needed the money and would be glad to give it to me since I seemed like a good person. I bashfully smiled and thanked him. He interrupted me, "I mean it, you've already treated me with more kindness and respect than I've received all week." Before I had a chance to get sentimental, he was right back to bartering. When he whipped out the gold watch for a second time I interrupted him, "Listen my friend, I don't have money, but again, I'm willing to get you some food. Are you hungry?"

At this he perked up, as if he hadn't heard me the first three times I offered. He smiled, took a four second pause and then continued, "Chinese restaurant right across the street. Let's go. It's cheap."

During the three block walk he told me about the deep unshakable sadness that his time in the Military had brought him. "They were white boys like you, but it didn't matter when you serve with folks for three years. You git closa den family. This was our first drop, we was out of the copter and in the air for no mo' than six seconds when bullets come shredding through the night. I get hit fo' times and I live." His voice was wavering, on the verge of tears again, "both my brothers.. both 'em get hit one time and they gone. It just ain't right. How do you fo'get sumin' like that? We landed and I had to hold their limp bodies in my arms. I can't fo'get. I try but I can't."

He wiped the tears now streaming down his face and we entered the restaurant. We ordered off of the menu and then sat down and waited for our food. It was a long time before the food came and even longer before we touched it. After about fifteen minutes of talking he reached across the table, grabbing my hand he said, "You know, you treated me tonight, better'n anybody else has in a long time." He got choked up as he told me, "I served this country fo twenty two years and then one day they just says 'Kirkman, thanks but seeya wouldn't wanna be yuh'. I try to be strong and smile, say hi hello how are you. Put on the right face but who cares about Mark?" His voice was wavering with pain, "Nobody cares." I squeezed his rough hand and said, "Mark, I care."

"It's so hard out here," he forced out through the tears. "Tonight...tonight before I met you I was lying on the freeway off ramp hoping to be run over. A big rig almost did. Last minute the driver saw me and he pulled off the road then up and pulled me off the road shouting at me."

I looked at him as a knot grew in my stomach. I didn't know what to say. I gave him a feeble smile; my attempt to assure him that everything would be all right.

"I'm so sad...I'm so sad, I'm soo sad" He squeezed my hand and repeated himself again; this time his words rumbled out from deep down from his soul and he lingered, emphasizing each word, "Paul, I'm so sad."

I mustered another weak smile with my mouth but my eyes reflected his, overflowing with pain and years of aimless wandering. He repeated himself one more time, "I'm so sad, Paul, I want to live, but I also want to die." Our eyes locked into a staring match then out of nowhere we both began to laugh. The conversation continued for another hour shifting between the serious and the absurd until the restaurant owner told us they were shutting down for the night.

Neither of us were ready for our time together to end so Mark said, "Come on, I know a little bar right down the street, we can get us a drink." I agreed and followed his lead.

We sat at a bar for hours and talked over a beer. The more I talked to him the more beautiful he became. I told him at one point, "Mark, I'm sorry dude but I definitely judged you at first, I mean I..."

He waved me off, "That's alright, we got past that... and all that is a part of the book."

"Right, and that book is your life?" I half questioned as the bar door creaked open and another homeless man hobbled in.

"Uhh huhhn, and then one day I was on the Southside and I met this guy and I fed him and did these wonderful things an..." The small frail looking man was now directly beside Mark, who asked, "How can I help you sir?"

Timidly the little guy held out and his hand "Hey sir, can you help a person out with a dollar fifty?"

"No, not at this particular time. I might talk to you in the future. Give me a minute; I'm talking with this guy." Barely audible, he responded, "Ok," and Mark then said, "Thank you, sir, 'preciate you." The door crept open and closed again and he was gone. There was a pause. I was waiting for Mark to speak up, "Look," he chuckled, "That's not a part of the book."

We laughed from our bellies, yet as we regained composure Mark said, "I'm a real simple man, I'm a real staff Sergeant in the army, and you got me because you showed me something genuine. I mean I was cryin. And you seen me crying. Real tears, and I'm so tough," he dropped his voice down to a rougher raspier tone, "and I can do all this," he comically bobbed around with his fists up in a fighter stance. "But its ok to feel sad, its ok, its Oh Kay. Real men... if you have feelins you can cry."

I laughed a little, "Right, it's when you can't that you need to be worried."

"Riggght, you got problems. So just cry. I didn't, I didn't wanna.. I'm sposed to be so tough. I was crying because I was in pain and real sad." The truth of the statement hovered for a moment and then out of nowhere he said, "I'm gunna show you something, young blood. Ima sign my name. You woulda never knew I could write like this."

He was like that; Mark had the amazing ability to keep the conversation moving, never lingering too long on any one topic. He made me feel very much at ease. He taught me how to be light, even in the darkness.

He finished up by writing his number below the message that read: "To a beautiful friend, I love you man."

He dropped his voice down, "That's how you get in touch with me. That's my mom's number; nobody gets that number. So, so, you can call me there."

The thought struck me, and I asked Mark, "What if I had decided not to talk to you tonight. I mean, what if I had decided to just keep walking, we wouldn't be here talking." He nodded. "Well, it's just uh..." I paused not wanting to imply anything negative.

"Come on speak it out, don't be uhhhing, we friends now. No uhhn's duhhs anz banz and nun o' that."

"Well, it's just that you turned that guy away earlier, and said he won't be part of the book. What if I had done that to you?"

He said, "Listen man, you can't walk down the street and take to heart every stupid comment made to you. There are opportunities all around us all day. You gotta draw the line and say nope, not gunna make that part of my book." Then in his gruff voice he comically said, "byee."

He looked me over for a moment, "I'm reading you, I get the feeling you have trouble telling people 'no'." I nodded. "You don't have to feel guilty. Look, if you don't have time, you don't have time. If you're doing something more important than you are doing something more important. We was put here together to talk and grow and laugh. Tonight God put us together, and we was busy." He studied me for a little while longer. "But that don't sit right wit cha do it? You prolly thankin, 'but Mark I can always make time.' But lemme ask you this, if you in the middla solvin' world hunger and somebody come up to you and say I'm hungry right now feed me, what you gunna do? Yuh might have to say nope sorry I can't help you right now."

I squinted, "So, it's about priorities?" He responded with an 'mm hmm'. That wasn't the last of the subject for the night, but for the moment we moved on. I asked him, "So, Mark, where do you stay?"

"I live in St. Charles with my brother. But I was in the hospital... dyin. I'm serious. I used the bathroom it was all blood coming out. So they give me a shot to stop it." Then he mumbled. "I'm sad about that, but I'm ok." He paused, scrunching his face in pain. In a wavering voice he continued, crying out, "I don't tell no body my pain I just keep it..." He waited, again choking back tears, "to me." He paused and sniffed, "Got a whole lot of it though," now chuckling. "I smile on the brokedest day. But I just keep it to myself. I act like every thangs just happy go lucky. Hey, ey, hey, how are yah and I'm so sad on the inside. Hey, you ever heard of the record by Smokey Robinson? It was called *Tears of a Clown*. It was a clown, and the reason why they called it *Tears of a Clown* was because the clown was crying on the inside. They called it *Tears of a Clown*, and it was by Smokey Robinson. It made him big money. But look what I'm sayin', don't be like me and hold it all in. Keep asking questions they're good but you gotta open up and let people in."

He then gave me advice on having healthy relationships, how to stay true to my beliefs, setting up boundaries as well as an incredibly insightful conversation about finding my purpose. He then casually said, "So you from Fort Lauderdale, right? Now I remember I was out there on the beach, and I had my big beach towel. I was layin' back and the rich people had them big ol' high buildings right there on the beach, and they'd look down with they cameras and telescopes and whatever, and so this white guy, he keep lookin down at me, and I had no idea. So he come down and he said, 'Sir where you from?' I toll him, 'I'm from St. Louis.' He said, 'I watch you every day.' I say, 'You doo?' He say, 'yes' he say, 'you don't have no one do you?'"

Mark's voice got emotional again, a combination of sorrow and joy. He continued, "I said no.' He said 'Well, I have something for you.' He gave me a big ol' bag with a big beach towel, gave me a bottled water and some chips, and he gave me a pair of shorts an pair a flip flops, and he gave me an envelope. He said, 'take this, I don't want you to open it right now.' I say, 'ok.' 'But I want you to spend it wherever you go. When I opened it, it had five hundred dollars in it. He said, 'I'm from Augusta, Georgia. I used to be homeless, and now I own my own steel factory. If anything ever happens to you I left my number. I want you to call me and let me know how you're doing.'" Mark smiled fighting back tears. "I said, 'how'd you know I needed your help?' He said, 'to tell you the truth, God sent you to me.'"

As the bar closed down that night, we were still not ready to part ways, since he had more to share, and I had more to learn. He said, "Now, what are you going to do tonight?" It was 2:30 am.

I suspected his original story about the car wasn't true. He was probably living in the streets. Even though it was late April, it was thirty degrees that night, and I did not want to leave him to sleep in the street. Frankly, I did not want to leave him at all. So I said, "Well, uhmm... find the car eventually."

"Find the car!" he exclaimed like a child being told on Christmas there was a new basketball hoop waiting outside.

"Yep, find the car. Yea, find the car. I have a car parked somewhere around Cherokee Street."

"Ahhuhh," in giddy anticipation, as he already knew he was getting an invite.

"Uhhm, thinking about sleeping in the car."

"You have a car?" again a childish joy in his voice.

"Yep".

"Yea you sleep in that car! And you turn that heat on! And eventually turn it off so you don't die, but yea!"

"You're welcome to join."

"You think I'm going to let you leave me? I burst into laughter and he continued, "I'll be that pit bull, that security dawg ahh watch yo self. Man I'll tell you what! God does some awesome things!"

So we started a 540 mile round trip, spontaneous road adventure to Chicago. During our drive time, I was blessed enough to have the foresight to record many of our conversations, and I look forward to writing a full novel to share our journey and more of the knowledge that Mark, my angel, brought to me. Initially, I thought God had put me in his path to help him, yet I see now that he was put in my life to help me. He developed my character, and altered the way I view the world and my fellow brothers and sisters.

Even with repeated visits back to the street where I met him and numerous unanswered calls to the number he gave me, I've never seen Mark since that night. However, his stories and his character have continued to impact me as the driving force for my desire to help the world to realize that everyone has value.

As humans, we make lots of unfounded assumptions.

If we can't give someone our time, we are making a judgment that our time is more valuable than theirs. This frustrates me.

If we were all created equally in the eyes of a Divine Creator, and I believe we were, it is our responsibility and should be our joy, to get to know our fellows. We never know when we might be having a conversation with, or entertaining an Angel!

About the Author

Paul Gruber's ability to empathize with others and understand what they are feeling was at one point a burden, when he was living just for himself and his own wants and desires. However, now that he has begun to live more for the service of others, that burden has turned to a blessing. His mission is to develop community action programs teaching skills that will empower people to create a self sustaining environment within residential communities.

God created us to be happy and by serving others a sense of happiness, personal fulfillment and gratitude arises. That feeling of having made a difference, empowering another to live a better life is one that ironically will change the life of the giver as well as the receiver.

Every heartfelt exchange of giving and receiving is a conversation that makes a difference!

Paul is in the process of writing his book which will contain more heartfelt stories like this one.

To connect with Paul, email him at
paulcgruber@gmail.com

A Soulful Conversation of Love and Gratitude

Teresa Velardi

Do you know the feeling of receiving a message in your heart that you just can't ignore? One that you can't explain to someone without seeming like you are a little bit wacky? It's a conversation with God. It's a knowing, a special kind of feeling in your soul that you have just received a message or an assignment that is completely attached to and in alignment with your purpose for being alive.

I have experienced these soul messages; actually I would call them soulful conversations. They are indeed conversations that have made a difference in my life, and in the lives of some others. The key to these conversations is to listen.

I'm a potter. I have a wonderfully creative gift in my hands that I believe is a gift from God. I knew the minute that I made that very first pot on the potter's wheel, that clay would forever be a part of my life. Throughout the years that I have been making pottery, I have created beautiful functional and decorative pieces. Although I do realize that they have beautified many a home, I don't believe that is the only purpose for me receiving the gift I have.

I also have a passion for feeding the hungry. By the grace of God, I've never gone hungry a day in my life, though millions of people have. Every day, people around the world starve to death, and in this day and age of abundance, it irritates me to no end that people are starving. Not only are

166

they starving in Africa and third world countries, they are starving in our own back yards.

I woke up one morning feeling as if I should do something that would generate some money in order to somehow make a difference in the lives of the hungry people in my own community. But how?

I had a studio full of clay that could be used to make bowls for an "empty bowls" project. My thought was to go to my church and ask if we could put together an event where local restaurants would donate soup, and we could have a soup supper. People would pay an amount at the door and they would receive a bowl which would be made by the hands of community members, then everyone would share in a meal of soup. That is the basic model for an "empty bowls" project.

The pastors at my church liked the idea, and we set a date for the event. They also enrolled someone who creates "ugly quilts". They are quilts that are made of old blankets and fabrics which are tied and sewn together to make sleeping bags. These finished "ugly quilt" sleeping bags are rolled up with a bag of toiletries and given to the homeless who live on the streets and under bridges in cities around the United States. The organization focuses on the cities where winter weather is harsh, and does its best to distribute them among the homeless in an effort to keep people from freezing to death. The event was going to be a night of service as well as soup. We called it "Soup, Sew and Share."

On a designated evening, I rolled out some clay and went to a gathering of some of the youth of my church community where they slumped the clay into paper bowls. The plan was that I would fire the clay bowls in the kiln once they were dry. I had about a dozen and a half bowls at the end of the night. As the bowls dried though, they began to crack. Sadly, many of them would be unusable. Well now, that didn't work very well, did it? The date of the event was coming up sooner than I would have liked, and now I needed another plan.

I went to bed that night asking God to give me a way to make the bowls that would be easy enough for the community to be involved in the project. I could have easily made a bunch of bowls on my potter's wheel on my own, but I wanted them to be made by the youth of the community. Hunger is a community issue, just one pair of hands will not solve it, and so I felt that this needed to be a community effort. Besides, what kid do you know who doesn't like to play with clay? I had willing hands waiting for my new idea.

After a few nights of asking God for his help, I woke up with these words swimming in my head. "It has to be circles and spirals." I asked, "What?" Again I heard, "It has to be circles and spirals!" Now, you might think I'm a little crazy hearing voices. I promise you, though, I heard those words. The voice was loud and clear. It wasn't a clearly audible voice; it was one that I heard in my soul. It was a voice that was kind and loving, yet firm in giving me a new direction. So, I got out of bed and went to my computer in search of the biblical meanings of circles and spirals.

The circle, as you might guess, is a symbol of never ending love. There is no break in a circle; it's a continuous line, continuous circular energy. Never ending love. Most married couples wear wedding bands as a symbol of their never ending love for each other. Okay, so I now knew the meaning of the circle and one part of the puzzle was solved... but spirals? I searched for the meaning, and could not find anything specific in the bible that would explain the meaning for the spiral. In my searching though, I learned that the spiral is found all throughout nature, like the way a rose blossoms in a spiral fashion. A multitude of sea shells are obvious spirals, large waves in the ocean move in a spiral motion. I've seen many a surfer tucked up inside the "curl" of the wave as it spirals its way to the shore. Plants break through soil reaching for the sunlight as they unfold in a spiral manner. Thorns on a cactus are lined up in a spiral. Weather patterns occur in spirals. As I looked, I was astonished at how many things in nature have a spiral motion to them. Our fingerprints are spirals. The universe itself is a spiral. I also know that there is a spiral motion that takes place in relationship to God. As we share his message and his love with others, I picture an outward moving spiral, as he draws us closer to him; I picture the spiraling motion being inward. I could see why the circle and the spiral needed to be a part of the bowls. I was on a Godly mission.

Then, I had a conversation with my good friend, Mikki. She had an organization called *With Gratitude and Grace*. I told her that I was going to launch this project and how it had come to be. When I told her that the bowls would be made of circles and spirals, she said, "Teresa, do you know that the spiral is the universal symbol for gratitude?" I nearly fell off my chair, and I began to cry. My heart was so touched with the realization that God was asking me to put a never ending supply of love and gratitude in these bowls.

Finally!! The message had been given to me defining what the other use of my hands would be in relation to the clay and the pottery. The bowl itself is a symbol of the ebb and flow of life, the fullness and then the emptying, the holding and the releasing, the giving and receiving. These representations are all contained within a bowl. And now, the bowls, which are metaphors for life itself, would be constructed of the representations of love and gratitude, the circle and the spiral. The message was clear! Life, no matter how full or how empty, should always be lived with love and gratitude.... always!

Now it was my job to find more hands, willing hands that would create these love and gratitude bowls. God had brought me this far on the journey, and I knew he would bring me to the next step.

I was meeting my good friend, Judy, for lunch one afternoon shortly after I got my 'assignment'. As I waited for her to finish a conversation on the phone, I got a little nudge. Another soulful directive. The Girl Scouts' area office was in this building. I told Judy I'd be right back, and went upstairs to see if I could enroll this service oriented organization to help in making the bowls. From previous interaction with the scouts, and having been a Girl Scout myself, I knew there was a pottery badge that could be earned by some of the girls, should they decide to help. And they did!! During a great conversation on how to bring this project to life, I had made a new friend in a woman whose name was.... are you ready for this? Grace! You tell me that God wasn't having a conversation with me the whole time I was working on this project.

I met Grace and three other Girl Scout leaders at a community center to discuss the logistics of our project. As we began our meeting, Grace indicated that it was standard practice to sing a Girl Scout song. So, I sang along to a song that was familiar to me.

Make new friends....But keep the old....One is silver and the other's gold.

That's the only verse I ever knew...so imagine my surprise when they kept on singing:

A circle is round...It has no end...That's how long I want to be your friend!

I stood there with my mouth open. I was shocked... once again I had received a message that I was in the right place with the right people. A circle is round, it has no end? Really? I didn't know whether to laugh or to openly cry tears of joy in release of the overwhelming feeling of gratitude I had in my heart at that moment.

So, needless to say, the Girl Scouts came through in a big way! We made about 100 bowls in 2 sessions! Every one of them was made with circles and spirals! As an added touch, I asked the girls to write a word on the bottom of the bowl that they created. It was to be their own word, a single word that described the feeling they had while making the bowl. They each knew what the bowl would be used for. Some of the words were "Peace", "Love", "Fun", "Gratitude", "Teamwork", "Grateful", "Service", "Harmony", "Vision" and so many more. It was wonderful to see the heart of each girl come through their hands as they created these precious bowls.

I glazed and fired the bowls in a bunch of different colors with the help of one of the older girls and displayed them the night of the soup supper. They went home with the families who had come out to share in the event. My heart was and still is full from this experience.

Recently, I got an invitation to display my pottery in a local studio/gallery. The woman who owns it asked me if I would be willing to do a project in the studio that could involve the community. She asked me if I had any ideas I could share...

You bet I do!!

So, during the winter sometime, we will be making the love and gratitude bowls again.

It is my vision to enlist and enroll pottery studios throughout the country to make the bowls and partner with local restaurants who will donate soup. The resulting soup supper will provide funds to food programs in their community that will benefit from the proceeds, and that will feed those who would otherwise go hungry. This project also builds stronger communities that will make a bigger difference. I believe that God is the potter and we are the clay, molded and shaped to do his good work.

If you have a pottery studio in your area that you can put me in touch with, I would like to have this conversation with that potter about taking this project into that community. It is certainly a conversation that is making a difference.

About the Author

Teresa Velardi is an author, speaker, potter and transformational life coach. She will take you on "Your Personal Transformational Journey", using pottery as an illustration for your own transformation from a ball of clay to a work of art! Along the way, you will learn how to unleash your power while connecting with your creative gifts and talents to live your most authentic life. Bring out the greatness within you as you discover that you already have the ability to shift every aspect of your life into high gear! Uncover your Dynamic Woman within and Wake Up to your most powerful, prosperous and passionate life.

See the Love and Gratitude bowls at http://bit.ly/TVPottery in the "Soup Sew and Share" photo album.

Learn more about Teresa at
www.teresavelardi.com and http://wakeupwomen.com/
Connect with Teresa at teresa@teresavelardi.com

Bless the Mess

Anna Banguilan

"She's gone Anna, Momma's gone!" It was my sister's familiar voice that said those words when I answered the phone on that day. I dropped to my knees, dropping my bags, with tears streaming down my face. My heart was in my throat, I didn't know what to say. I was in shock. It would be the coldest weekend in Tennessee and it would be followed by one of the coldest years of my life.

It was Sunday, December 11, 2005, when I got that call. The thoughts rattled in my head! *What could I have done?* She wasn't sick, just the typical aches and pains of getting older. *Why did I pick this weekend to take a holiday?* I had just talked to her and she was going to be at my house the following week to help me with a big project. *Why? Why? Why?* Then I thought, *I have to go home and get the dog, feed the cats! How far is it to Alabama? Oh, my dad, I need to talk to my dad!*

The 15 hour drive was so surreal, I barely remember. My partner, Stephanie, and I stopped to see my cousin in South Carolina and get some hugs. I so needed those hugs! We stopped in Atlanta just long enough to pick up the dog.

Two days after receiving the news, I was standing in my Momma's kitchen watching family and friends fill the house. I could feel the love and laughter lifting my soul. I had a sense of my Mom being there and being so happy. I felt as if she were wearing my hands like gloves as I rinsed the dishes in the sink. I felt her hug me and, for the moment, I am at peace.

After returning home two days later, I locked myself in the bathroom at my studio. I was heartbroken. I couldn't think and I couldn't work. I was crying and hitting the walls, calling out to God and asking, "Why me, God? Why me?"

Today, I can say that I took my Mother's passing personally. I was so focused on it that nothing else really mattered at the time. My saving grace was my son being born six months after my mom's passing. My mother was my number one cheerleader and always told me I could do anything I put my mind to. She was usually right there beside me to cheer me on and help me out. For the next two years I was in a state of depression, grief and numbness. I was deciding whether to stay or go. I didn't want to be here without my Mom. I was fighting my very existence while people I loved could only stand by and offer their support and love, only to have me throw it back in anger and frustration.

I was the happy one, the silly one, and that person was gone. She left with my mother. I bless the people who saw me through that time, for them to love me that much to stick by me and hold me when I didn't want to be held.

I allowed my business and my relationships to wane. I had mixed thoughts of '*oh shit*' and '*I don't care!*' I woke up each morning with anxiety as if someone were pulling me up by my shirt, yanking me up and out of sleep, I gulped for breath and hated that I was still on the planet. I had a list of things I had to do in an effort to patch up all the things that were happening, and then letting it all go. I was spiraling out of control.

I was the "fix it" person, I was the one who everyone relied on and I was stumbling. How do you fix this? I kept thinking, if I could back up time (control Z, control Z) to the days before her death. If I could just go back to the last conversation where we were yelling through the phone, "I LOVE YOU" "I can't wait to see you!" If I could go back to the last time I saw her at my brother's house, I could feel the hugs, the glorious Momma hugs! I remember being curled up in a ball on the floor, tired, exhausted, angry and sad. I was hearing in my head, "You are so selfish, this didn't just happen to you, it happened to so many others, too!"

What do you do when God takes away one of your favorite people?

I moved my studio to get away from the memories. I had expanded and given up on my businesses all at the same time, not very appreciative of the people who were attempting to keep it afloat and feeling sick every morning when I pulled up in front of the building. Nothing really mattered and I was stuck in my muck! By November 2007, I was exhausted! I stepped out onto my back deck and yelled up to God, either take me off the earth or give me an answer because I give up!

Two days later, the answers came for me in an early Holiday present from my partner's mom. It is the book, "The Astonishing Power of Emotions," along with the CD, "Death and Life," by Abraham-Hicks. I can say that these 2 items saved my life. I read this book and listened to the CD several times over the course of the next few weeks. A light bulb went off as I realized that I create my own reality and everything we know IS energy! The biggest ah-ha was this: If I become lighter, energetically, I can communicate with my mom. My understanding is I AM energy and, as energy, I vibrate on a certain frequency. When I am sad, I am a heavier vibration and emitting a different frequency than when I am happy and emitting a lighter vibration. When I learn to shift how I feel in any situation, I can change my vibration and this changes my frequency and I can get a different result.

You see, my knowing is when we perceive people as dying, they are actually just releasing their heavier denser human form and their energy never dies. Call it spirit, soul, Source; they are lighter and vibrating on a higher frequency and this means when I am happy, I am lighter and I can talk to my mom. This concept sounded a bit "woo-woo" to me to me AND I was willing to try it! I had 2 choices, die or get happy. I chose happy!

I embrace a daily conversation with myself that starts the moment I wake up. I ask myself, what do I appreciate today? I also ask, what do I have to celebrate today? I do a morning meditation and often write down my thoughts. One morning I woke up hearing my mom's voice, I felt as if I had been talking with her all night. From that point forward I have sensed her energy with me daily. I have had amazing conversations with her in meditation and in the time I spend just sitting still. Sometimes, I even find myself laughing out loud when chatting with her. She is still here with me, with all of us, and we can communicate with her when we allow it. She has even helped me through traffic, think about it, she has the aerial view; just ask Ruth to get you through traffic, then be quiet and listen. She usually makes you follow Hondas or a dark forest green car. When she was still here with us, she drove a dark green Honda CRV. My mother's energy opened up a way for my guides to communicate with me and I journal messages. I often get answers to my own questions.

I was so excited about understanding human beings as energy. It is a thought I have had since I was 16 years old, I just never said anything to anyone about it. I wanted to share it with everyone. What I realized in my waking up to this awareness is that not everyone is ready for this information. Many of my friends thought I had truly gone over the deep end as I told them my story and shared how they have absolute control over their lives. I soon started searching for people to talk to and joined a short-lived mastermind group. In the few times that we met, I was given the message, "soften the information for the masses." I didn't really understand that message until years later. I studied Reiki. I call it an energy wellness modality. I use Reiki in my own meditation and also work with family and friends. Reiki is what I call a universal energy exchange.

In 2008 I created a group on meetup.com called "The Atlanta Law of Attraction and Creativity Group." My intention in creating this group was to attract like-minded people and have conversations where people weren't rolling their eyes or glazing over as I talked about how everything is energy. Our group was meeting weekly for about a year when I received an email from someone who liked what I had on my group page and just wanted to have a conversation. We set up a time to talk. He introduced himself as Tre Black. We spent 45 minutes talking about all of my mentors, my art, Reiki, poetry and my group. Then, he told me that he and his partner, Lis were launching a radio station, *Source Energy Radio*, at the end of 2009 and he asked me if I would like to have a radio show! I was nervous and, at the same time, I was excited! I said I would "give it a shot".

On September 23, 2009, I did my first radio show called "Bless the Mess." Tre and Lis were thrilled and I continued to record shows several times a week to be aired on the station. During my conversations with Tre, I thought about becoming a life coach. Tre used to ask me, "Why do you need external validation for something you know you already are?" I realized that I was insecure about all the new awareness I was receiving and the changes in my life. Doing the radio shows really helped me to validate who I was becoming.

I created radio shows on Source Energy Radio for 6 months when Tre passed on from the physical and, with that, Source Energy Radio was no longer airing. I never got the opportunity to meet Tre in person. We only spoke through Skype and on the phone and I can say that he profoundly changed my life. He helped me see that I could be of great service and share not only my message, but the messages of others as well.

Tre is also an energy that is with me constantly and guides me in so many profound ways. In May 2010, I was debating on traveling to NYC to share in a meetup group there and Tre's memorial party. I received validation when I received a gifted intuitive reading from someone I had never physically met. Tre was coming through loud and clear. One message was, "carry the dream." I was told that, "We stopped and he never stopped." At the time of this intuitive reading, I had received a thought to register the name *Universal Energy Radio* and start recording. Tre had taught me some things about audio recording and constantly pushed the idea of content.

I wasn't really sure how I was going to create this station...I just did it. July 1, 2010, Eliza Bill, another former source Energy Radio Host, and I launched Universal Energy Radio . It currently airs live daily and podcasts to iTunes. At the time of the launch there were two of us on a few times a week. I soon recruited my cousin, a numerologist, and few others to co-create with me. I have had the opportunity to share the airwaves and have conversations with some amazing individuals whose vision is to uplift, share and hold space for others. I love the idea that there are so many unique perspectives in the world as each individual is unique.

Over the course of the next few years I have opened myself up to infinite possibility. I did get certified as a life coach, it's just that human part of me wanting validation. Tre chuckles at this. I have downsized my business and upsized my awareness. I have nurtured my relationships and have been perfectly fine when I realize that friends, clients, even family members, drift away. I understand that every human being is on their own journey and since we are all energy, we can ebb and flow like water in the ocean. The friendships and relationships I have now are richer and conversations are more delicious. I see my children, now ages 4 and 7, as my best teachers and love them unconditionally.

I truly understand myself. In this understanding, I am also knowing that I am the best me for me first. Then I can be the best me for everyone else around me. I am the example. I do not have to force any of my beliefs on anyone. As I further understand Law of Attraction, I find myself in the midst of people with similar beliefs. I have conversations about Law of Attraction. It is the universal law that states, what you focus on expands. You must understand that it is energy first, everything you want is created energetically first and then it materializes. Do you ever wonder why you get "sort of" what you wanted and not exactly what you wanted? Vibration and frequency have to meet up with vibration and frequency, before exactly what you wanted can come to be.

I have been an entrepreneur for 27 years. As I look back at my life, I have noticed times when I thought I was doing things "by the seat of my pants". Now I know that these are the times I was truly guided. I took risks, I created, and I succeeded. It was the conversations with my mom in person, and her belief in me, that kept me going. I remember when I was tired and not happy about my business, she told me to let it go. I thought I was responsible for those around me and their livelihood. It took her passing for me to wake up to the realization that if I am beholden to a job or a business just for money, I am going to have a miserable life.

As I move forward, there are several conversations that stand out. I recognize that they have helped me shift my mindset and have allowed me to let go. I was blessed to have a month of monks on my radio station. As they spoke, I realized that you can let go of your suffering in a moment, as you are the one holding it in place. You choose the stories you bring with you and, as you tell those stories, you bring the energy and emotion with you into your NOW. It is so important to understand this because your NOW is how you create. Your NOW energy creates your tomorrow, your next week and your next month. You can tell how your tomorrow will be based on how you FEEL right NOW.

I can tell my story and not get emotional in a sad, depressed, angry way. As you read my story how do you feel?

Did you go through a range of emotions? Check into that and notice what you notice. I remember staying with my dad a few months after my mom's passing. I went to check up on him as he wasn't sleeping very well. I peeked into his room and he was asleep and on the pillow next to him were Mom's glasses. I broke down and wept. Again, my heart felt pierced. Now I tell that story and it is not a sad one. It is a story of my dad, my hero, who loved my mom so much. He continues to live in the house they had built, her dream home, on the property she inherited from her father. Her energy is there, we hang out with her under her magnolia tree in the back yard.

My conversations with my Dad are so beautiful, he is amazing. He lives life fully and I have gotten to know this person who is so much more than my dad. He shares books, he shares his thoughts knowing that my mom wants him to be happy and keep living his beautiful life.

I have been gifted so much in my shifting. When I let go of money as the only way to receive, my world opened up. As Dr. David Ault says, "solution already exists," you just have to tap into it. I have always been a "how" person. If you were someone in my life who wanted to create something, you came to me. My business has been graphic design, print, promotions, advertising and marketing and, although I realize these are fun, this is not where my passion lies. I really want people to understand that they are so much more than what they see in the mirror. They have amazing power and the ability to live an amazing life and as I say this I think of HOW I can get this across? The answer is: Be the example. I also know that you have to come from your heart and live truly in your heart space.

A mentor and dear friend, Don Milton, a life and freedom coach, really help me realize that even though I was on my journey, I was still trying to figure out 'how'. Don says, "Don't argue with Source." Allow yourself to open up and allow Source, your higher self, to do the work. You have to be open to what shows up. Don also helped me clear some issues I still had around my mother's passing by using a technique called matrix re-imprinting. My conversations and sessions with Don helped me let go of some stuck sadness and bring more joy and love into my heart. I thought when I woke up to my awareness, it couldn't get any better and I realize it always gets better and better every day and in every way.

There is always more to learn and experience. Every human being has their own unique perspective and even though we may be similar, no two are alike. This world is full of so many beautiful and amazing beings. We all have ideas and plans and we are taking inspired action in co-creating an infinite universe with infinite possibility. I say "Bless the Mess!" Bless all of the messes because without the messes we wouldn't change, grow, expand, look the other way, find ways to feel better or seek out others to co-create with us on our journey. Choose to bless the mess so, as you go through it, you wake up to possibility in it and shift how you feel in it. This changes everything; it's Universal Law.

On my journey, I have experienced so much. At times, I realized I was comfortably uncomfortable and things had to change. I have stepped out of my comfort zone many times. I have hired coaches, read books, taken workshops, gotten acupuncture, Reiki and massage. I've done some standup comedy and really gotten transparent with my life. No more stuffing down, no more fixing everything for everyone. That's not my job. I allow people to be who they are. I share this information when asked about it and I go about my day to day life shifting my thoughts and asking, "How does it get any better than this?"

You get to choose, it's your life, not your kids, or your parents, or your spouse, or anyone else for that matter. Realize that when you choose to be the best you for you first, everyone around you wins; you are calmer, more peaceful and you will be able to *interact* versus *react* in any situation. It is a process and as my alchemy teacher, Pam Rennie, says, "Notice what you notice," because in the moment you notice the shifting, you have already become more.

About the Author

Anna Banguilan has spent the majority of her professional life as a graphic artist, textile printer, promotions and marketing expert. As an entrepreneur, she is always experiencing the fabulous roller coaster ride we call life.

Her life changed dramatically in 2005 with the death of her mother. This event made her look up and out to become "more". In the search for the answers to her questions, she was given a copy of *"The Astonishing Power of Emotions"* by Abraham-Hicks and found a new "bliss" of creating her own new reality and helping others do the same.

Anna is the founder of *Universal Energy Radio* and now adds to her repertoire, radio talk show host, law of attraction facilitator and life coach, Reiki master, speaker and author.

"Life is a journey, be happy where you are and watch where it takes you!"

Learn more about Anna and *Universal Energy Radio* at: http://universalenergyradio.com/ and http://lifegetsbetterandbetter.com/

Connect with her at: Anna@lifegetsbetterandbetter.com

Conversations That Are Out of Sight

Patricia Giankas

Before I was 18, I lead a very sheltered life. Unknown to my family, I was also a victim of abuse. Even though those experiences were filled with negativity, they led me to my spirituality. Through that, I learned to believe in myself and to love myself. I learned to change my thought process. I have been able to detach from the sad, negative, upsetting and unforgiving thoughts. I put them in what I call a thought bank, a kind of emotional bank account where thoughts are consciously converted from negative to positive.

Your thoughts are your own to consciously convert from negative to positive. When nurtured, your thoughts put you on a happiness path. Since we are what we think, this process allows us to detach ourselves from, and let go of, all negative thoughts, enabling us to become the people we really want to be.

As I think of who it is that I aspire to be, I have to take into consideration many conversations that have happened thorough out my life that, for some, may seem as if they are out of sight.

Although I don't remember much before the age of 5, I do know that my ability to encounter my deceased family and friends actually began at that age. These encounters happened throughout my childhood, like the experience I had with a vase falling from a high place as I reached to get it. Someone was there to keep it from falling. There was no one else in the room, yet I had help. As I reflect back to when I was 18 and pregnant, I can recall seeing a person standing at my bedside smiling down at me. She was wearing a white gown and her long, beautiful black hair cascaded across her body. I remember wondering why she was there. I found out the next day that one of my aunts had passed away. Had she come to visit me?

Years later another one of my aunts, who wanted to wait until she was 90 years old before leaving this physical world, was planning her own earthly departure. I think she planned it perfectly, because within days of her 90th birthday, she did an amazing thing. On the Thursday after she turned 90, my aunt had a conversation with my father and my uncle, her two brothers, telling them that if anything should happen to her, she didn't want to be put on any artificial means of life support. Ten minutes later, after finishing her dinner, she walked away from the kitchen to go upstairs, as she always had. The door to the basement, which had never been kept open, was open. As she walked near the door, my aunt had a massive stroke and fell face first down the stairs.

When the ambulance came, she appeared to be comatose. The paramedics immediately put tubes down her throat, and took her to the hospital. We were all waiting there when she arrived since my cousin's wife had called the family to report what had happened. Two doctors came in to update the family on what was happening. My dad and uncle were trying to get the message across on behalf of my aunt. "Please tell them to let her go. She is not here. She is gone." We were confused by their attempts to resuscitate her.

Just an hour before they unplugged the life support, my Aunt and my Grandmother "visited" my father. He saw them walking in his bedroom. They had come to visit him.

The following Friday, I was to spend some time with a friend. I had to tell her that my aunt had just passed away and we would have to reschedule. My friend, Audrye, who I met a few months before, said "Your aunt is on a raft and she cannot speak. She doesn't understand the language she is speaking." My aunt spoke Creole English. Audrye shared that my aunt had told her that she was trying to get used to her new surroundings. She also had a message for my father that he would be fine and not to worry. My aunt also sent a message confirming that my business would do extremely well, that she would be there for me and I should not worry. My cousin was in the car with me when Audrye gave me the messages. She began weeping. Just the week before, her mom had said that she wanted to go on a raft. What were the chances of this happening?

The week before my aunt's passing, her granddaughter was due to have her baby. She was way past her due date, and then at 3:00 that morning, she gave birth to a little girl. She named that baby girl after my aunt, who was the source of my family. She kept all the family members grounded together with an invisible "cord".

Although my aunt never spoke fluent English, and had a difficult time expressing herself in a way that others could understand, she knew she wanted to live until she was 90. She also knew that when she died, she didn't want to experience pain or suffering. She wanted to leave this earth quickly. Her passing was just as if she had planned it all to happen as it did. Her name will live on with her granddaughter.

I knew my aunt loved me very much. Every time she would go back to her homeland she would bring me a pair of gold earrings. It was and is the little things that we remember about the relationships we have with those we love and who love us. If I could choose just one thing that I would like to pass on to others, it would be this; I want to give people comfort. I want them to take comfort in knowing that there are telltale signs as the time draws near for a loved one to pass on. I encourage you to stop, take a breath, listen and look. Don't take things for granted, because these things are part of the story of our loved ones telling us that there is an afterlife. We can help each other, console each other through the grieving process, and we can also share in the knowing that our loved ones have gone somewhere where they really want to be.

A week prior to my aunt's passing, I read a book about our thoughts and thought processes. It explained that when we die, the invisible cord to this body is broken and is separated from the soul body, or etheric body. Our thoughts go with us, and for the first couple of days after passing, we spend time reflecting about out life before we make the journey from this realm. Whatever we want to create, we can. I've started to encounter many different things and many people who can explain things about the afterlife. Knowing this information has given me peace.

Have you ever felt as though you are being directed to certain people who would make a huge difference in your life? A friend of mine introduced me to Beth Johnston of the International Women's Leadership Association. A few months later, we met in person and we just hugged. There was great energy between us and I knew that Beth would be someone who would make a difference in my life. I have since been featured in her magazine and so many doors have opened for me since I met her. Beth has a passion for helping women to be successful, and radiates the most positive energy. She told me about the un-conference taking place in Florida and thought it would be a good idea for me to attend, so I booked my ticket. Having been to so many conferences in my life, I was a little apprehensive and had some doubt that it would really benefit me to go. I made the trip anyway.

I stayed with a friend before the start of the conference. I was aware of a strange energy in the room I would stay in, and my friend had someone come to the house to remove what she called a "dense energy." The next night, I heard a loud voice say, "Clear Communications." I wasn't quite sure what that meant or whether the time I heard it, 2:05 was significant. I wondered if it had anything to do with angels so I looked up "angel 2:05" on the Internet and this is what I read, "You can be confident that all the changes you are living through are heavenly controlled. It's essential for you to stay positive and slowly move forward on your life path. Optimism and positive vibrations emitting from deep inside of you will guarantee the best possible outcome of all the changes." I find it interesting that I can experience these things. And as time goes by, I experience them more often.

When I arrived at the conference, the first person I met was Audrye. She's the friend I mentioned earlier who was giving me messages from my aunt right after she had passed away. We became friends very quickly. I think she is such a beautiful, kind person. She's an angel. Later that day, while Audrye was giving me a reading, she said that I was starting to open up my spiritual side. Since the visit of my aunt while I was pregnant years earlier, the reading I had done on the afterlife, and what I was experiencing on my own in feeling the nature of particular energies, I was very curious to know more.

I have experienced many tragedies in my lifetime, physically, emotionally and financially. I've been a millionaire two times and lost it two times over, and the recent message from my aunt assures me that I will succeed again and that my business will be great. I intuitively knew that I needed to turn to spiritualism, something I started to pursue years ago. I know there are things I need to learn.

After my meeting with Audrye, we chatted on the way downstairs. Along the way we met another woman who also gave me a great reading and did an exercise with me that opened my chakras. I was then able to see things like I have never seem them before. I drew pictures of many things during the time she spent with me. One of the pictures was of me in a well with a beautiful crown on my head and I was wearing a cloak with many jewels. As I looked up, I saw the sun. (When I returned to the office after the conference, I drew my vision on the board in my office. One of the girls commented that it looked like Joseph's cloak of jewels.) Interesting. I had several other visions, and although I don't know what they mean yet, I'm hopeful that the meaning of each will be revealed to me.

Later on, while at that conference, I made a third connection. The universe seems to be placing all of these powerful women in my life, each having a message for me. I am absorbing the information and the messages like a sponge. None of them know what the other has said to me, yet they are all telling me almost the same thing.

Since I have returned home from that event, I am able to see auras of people. I'm not sure what all the colors mean yet, but I look up the meanings. I really can't believe that I can actually see this. I want to know what is going on around us, and what is really going on when our life on this earth is over.

I have been having some interesting dreams. In them, I have climbed mountains receiving help to cross over from a man whose face I could not see. I have floated on beautiful clear water and not gotten wet, and that same man was beside me. I've dreamed of Jesus Christ walking along the road holding my hand on more than one occasion. I've walked with him as he is wearing a white flowing gown near three lamp posts. I have had many dreams where I see a hand stretching out to hold mine to walk me through my journey.

I leave you with the thought that there is an eternal conversation going on out of our human sight and we are forever and always connected to Spirit. I am amazed at the beautiful thoughts that have come to me through my encounters with those who have gone on before me. I will keep them as cherished possessions in my thought bank. I can make additional deposits into my positive emotional bank accounts as I reflect on the beauty of this life, and that which is yet to come...

About the Author

Patricia Giankas brings over thirty years of experience in the Financial Services industry; leveraging her expertise and know-how. She recognized the need for offering clients complete financial representation. She has been recognized in her field of expertise and has established a reputation as the true expert and leader in the mortgage industry.

Patricia's new found ability to connect with her dreams and to those family members and friends who have passed on has totally intrigued her. She is exploring ways that she can share her message of hope with people who are grieving for those they have loved and lost. This story is dedicated to the memory of Patricia's Aunt Finee.

Patricia has lectured at women shelters and the YWCA. She has provided assistance to community charities, bringing hope and help to various areas of the world. In this time where many people are turned upside down in their finances, Patricia helps them to make sense of their financial mess.

Connect with Patricia at p.giankas@score-up.ca
and http://www.score-up.ca/

From Ph.D. to Setting Angels Free

Elizabeth Locey, Ph.D.

*"When You Sing Your Truth Song, Imprisoned Angels
Are Set Free"*

Have you ever walked into a room with a firm conviction about how the world works, and walked out having been turned inside out and upside down?

I have. Believe me, it's never something that you *want* to do, but it's a *good thing*.

I walked into a counseling session back in 2001, never expecting to have my belief system flipped on its head, instantaneously.

After all, I was a university professor. I knew what I knew. And what I knew was that everything that existed could be proven and accounted for. My Ph.D. in French Literature and Women's Studies had drummed out all the voices that had whispered to me as a child about fairies, magic and what exists beyond the clouds.

So at the end of our session, when my therapist-friend changed seats and said, "Elizabeth, I don't know how you're going to take this, but what I'm about to share with you has become a big part of my life." I thought she was going to tell me that she was getting divorced or had been diagnosed with a major illness.

What I did NOT expect was:

"I've started channeling an entity named Michael, and he wants to say hi."

Wait, did she just say *"channeling an entity?!??!?"*

My initial response would normally have been to snort. Guffaw. Roll my eyes.

As an intellectual, I knew in my *bones* that so-called "channeling" and all that New Age B.S. was for manipulating weak-minded people. And because I loved my friend, I wasn't going to mock her. I was, however, going to leave. I might have to re-evaluate our friendship, but first I needed to get out of there before any snorting or eye-rolling started.

As I was getting up, the needle on the unexpected meter moved to MAX.

Suddenly, the energy in the room shifted like I've never felt anything shift before or since. It was like an Atomic Bomb of Love was dropped in the room. The blast field knocked me back into the seat and pinned me there, wide-eyed.

Suddenly, my friend was no longer recognizable. In front of me was someone who definitely was NOT her. Someone older, wiser...*stranger*! Someone who was performing a rapid-fire comedy routine of pure love.

Suddenly, I no longer knew which way was up. Like gravity ceased to exist in that moment. The laws of physics and everything I knew to be true suddenly came undone.

In that instant, I went from thinking, no...knowing! that channeling was bull**** to actually knowing that it was *real*. Although my friend's physique was not dramatically changed in the process, it was clear to me that she was no longer completely alone in her body. Her presence was different.

Whoa.

Little did I know, walking out of that room dizzy but grinning from ear to ear, that I would be channeling an entity myself about four months later.

His name was "Georgie". He was a healer. And... he was a walrus. I knew whenever he wanted to "come in" because I would feel my nose twitch and my cheeks move apart to make room for his tusks. You might think that's weird, but having someone or something else take over your body and use your voice, your eyes, your hands, and your feet for a while is pretty weird, too. Once you get over that, anything goes. The tusks just came with the package.

My "Georgie" period lasted for about two years. As soon as I started channeling, my friend suggested we stop seeing each other in the professional setting as therapist and client and that we start having lunch every Friday. Those weekly lunches were a true education. Without knowing it, I was honing my intuition every time I sat across from her.

Truth Teller

Fast forward another five years. I had gotten married, had a daughter, and been tenured and elevated to the rank of Department Chair.

One day in April 2008, as I was pulling out the chair to sit opposite my friend at our favorite gourmet pizza place, she looked more radiant than usual. She leaned over the table to grab me: "Elizabeth! I've just had my Akashic Records read, and you've GOT to do it. This is for you!" she blurted out, breathlessly.

I threw up my hands. Hold on! I didn't even know what those... What were they? A-what-ish records? I didn't know what they were, much less pronounce it. And...I wasn't going to do them, either. In part because I'm the kind of person who, for better or for worse, immediately digs in her heels to say no whenever someone says I "have to" do something.

Yep. There I was, once again resisting the major shifts my friend presented to me on a silver platter.

And frankly, I wasn't in the mood to spend money on myself. At that moment, my beautiful 2-year-old daughter was in a body cast. She had broken her leg in the park on the first nice spring day. At this point, we had plenty of new medical bills on top of the massive medical debt we had accrued two years before. You see, my daughter was born at 27 weeks, weighing just over a pound and a half. She had spent her first 3 months in the NICU. Don't worry though, today she's a gorgeous, smart, bi-lingual and very active first grader who loves to draw, do ballet and play soccer.

Fortunately for me and for all the people I help these days, my friend and mentor wouldn't let me off the hook.

She insisted. In fact, she wouldn't even let me order lunch—*our* lunch—until I said I would. And I'm so glad she did.

The Akashic Records, by the way, contain your soul's blueprint. They're an ethereal library holding the energetic imprint of everything that has ever happened, or is likely to happen, to you and everyone else, both in your current lifetime, and all of your past lifetimes as well. They contain Records for every person, place, thing, idea, institution, date and event. You name it, and you'll find it in the Records.

It's held safe and secure by Keepers or Guardians who won't let others in without your permission to learn things about you that *you* don't even know. All major religions make reference to this phenomenon, and in the Judeo-Christian tradition it's called the Book of Life, where your deeds are inscribed so that you can be sent to heaven or hell on Judgment Day. Except, as someone who visits these Records daily, I can tell you that there's *no* judgment there, just pure love.

When someone has a near-death experience and "sees her life flash before her eyes," that's her still-living human brain connecting with the trillions of pieces of information in her Record. I think this is where our Higher Selves live/hang out. I also think this is where we go back to at the end of our lives.

Intuition and Akashic Records are virtually the same thing, but differ in scale and accessibility. Intuition is information from your Akashic that is carefully ladled out to you by your Higher Self *exactly* when you need it. Still, it's hard to get intuitive hits about what you want to know when you want to know it. That's what Records channels or consultants are for.

A few weeks after that fateful lunch, I was sitting in my car with a cell phone to my ear and a list of questions on a clipboard propped against the steering wheel. I couldn't do this from my office because students and faculty were constantly walking in unannounced. And I couldn't do it from home, because I didn't want my deepest answers from my *soul*—the ones I didn't even know yet—to be overheard by my husband, who shared my former beliefs about metaphysics.

From my first question, I was hooked. My life was again changed in ways I could not-have imagined. From the get-go, my first conversation with my Akashic Record *really made a difference* in my life.

The answer made me cry because it was so gorgeous, and also confused me for years.

Q: *"Who am I on a soul level?"*

A: *"You are a Truth Teller, with capital T's. And when you sing your Truth song, imprisoned angels are set free."*

That answer made me feel warm and alive and grateful and recognized. And yet nowhere did I feel as if I knew where to *be* the Truth Teller. How did that fit in my life as a French professor and department chair?

I walked away from a "brilliant career" and a guaranteed salary for life. Within twenty months of this first channeling, I resigned from my academic position. I'd had several other channelings in between, and my heart was broken on the third one, when I asked if *I* could learn to channel Records myself. My Keepers told me that I had "bigger fish to fry:" that the rug was about to be pulled out from under me and I needed to pay attention.

Sure enough, two months later, when I announced I was stepping down as chair, my new dean and president decided, without telling anyone, to shut our department down! By the time my term ended, my department did not exist anymore. I was bitter, felt betrayed, and had a strong sense that the university life I had always lived, and always *wanted* to live, was forever soured.

I was an award-winning professor; a respected scholar in my field, known both in the U.S. and abroad for my book, articles and presentations. At age 35, I was made department chair on the same day that I was installed into the #3 position in my international professional organization. I was a shining example of the successful young academic and I walked away from it all in the middle of the worst economic downturn in the US in 75 years.

And I'm *so* glad I did.

May 15, 2010 was my last day as a professor. My first visit to my Akashic Record was May 18, 2008. Boom.

Today, just a few years later, I have created a thriving global practice as a spiritual business coach and Akashic Records channel for change-agents.

That's right! I'd heard the Keepers wrong; they hadn't said "no" to me channeling Akashic Records; what they really meant was "not now."

These days I help entrepreneurs and business leaders all over the world to find their intuitive edge and brilliant answers to move them forward powerfully and quickly, so that they can help the world become a better, healthier, more supported, more connected, more empowered and more joyful place.

And you know what? The Q & A format of the way I channel the Records means that each session is a conversation that makes a difference; a profound and lasting difference in the lives of my clients and the lives of those whom they touch.

On a busy day, I can start as many as five conversations that make a difference—five waves of change around the world.

And that feels really *g-o-o-d*. As it turns out, I *love* setting imprisoned angels free.

So, as a Truth Teller, here are some things you should consider about your life, Planet Earth and the Universe:

You're here for a reason.
Find out why, and then go *do something* about it.

You know more than you think you do.

I promise.

You are *Divine.*

A perfect being full of Love. One moment at a time, I invite you to start living in your divinity rather than your humanity. See what that feels like. No self-judgment allowed if you can't do it 24/7; if you could, you wouldn't be here anymore, right? I bet you're gonna love it!

Everything is energy.

Einstein teaches us that everything is energy. All energy is located somewhere on a Love-to-fear spectrum. I like to call the Love end the "Abundance Zone." This is where things like generosity, acceptance, fun, laughter, truth, faith, connection, wisdom, intuition, imagination, expansion, luck and basically all good things are located. Giving is here, and so is receiving.

On the other hand, the Scarcity Zone is all about *stopping* the flow. Behaviors like hoarding or not daring to give or receive are located here. Scarcity isn't just about clinging to what you've got, fear, or anxiety; it's also about overwhelm, judgment of self and others, jealousy, greed, pain, depression, doubt, anger, struggle and control.

Surrender and giving up are opposite energies.

Surrendering the "how" to the Universe or your Higher Self is the best way to get things done, and is one of the highest-frequency actions you can ever take. Giving up— being defeated and losing hope—is one of the lowest-frequency energies out there. Know the difference and act accordingly.

Co-creation (surrendering the how + taking right action) is the best way to get anything you want.

Don't let your ego-brain fool you into thinking you know better than the Universe! I'm not proud to say that I've done this, but I have. I'm a *recovering* control freak.

Your human vision is very short-sighted.

When you experience something like a job loss or a disease, you are likely to see it as "tragic," whereas in reality it's just *Step One of giving you exactly what you want.* Accept that it's not the full story, just the opening chapter. The story is never over, so stop judging it and freaking out; just let it go and go with the flow.

Struggle is nothing more than you trying to stand against the combined wisdom of the entire divine Universe.

This sounds kind of silly for you to do that when put this way, right? It's like one mosquito trying to hold back all the wind in the world; it's very tiring and completely futile. And consider this: who do you think knows better—the wind, or the mosquito?

Apply the 80/20 Rule:

You do 20% of the work by taking the actions you are guided to take, and leave the other 80% to the Universe. It will create and deliver all of the brilliant ideas, all the finding of correct partners and setting them right in front of you, all the good "luck," the fabulous opportunities, everything. It knows exactly how to fulfill your wildest dreams, and will bring them to you quickly if you'll just get out of the way!

The Universe loves you and wants you to be happy.

Look for the presents that it brings you every day. The more you open your eyes to see the gifts, and express gratitude for them, the better your life will get and the more presents you'll see... everywhere.

Contrary to what you've been taught, this is not a zero-sum game.

There are infinite resources available to those who choose to see them. And infinite support. We live in an abundant Universe.

Gratitude is an anti-inflammatory.

Slather it liberally on relationships, situations or emotions that are getting tight or heating up in an uncomfortable way. Like a lubricant, it makes everything work more smoothly. It even works on pain. Try applying gratitude the next time you get a headache before reaching for the Advil.

Use your intuition!

Why cut yourself off from the most clairvoyant and powerful (= divine) part of you? Intuition helps you to be in the right place at the right time, and to say and do the right things to help you get exactly what you want. In my world, it's foolish to turn your back on this amazing resource which doesn't cost a single cent to use. And if you're already using your intuition; great! Now go use it *more.*

Stay grounded.

I know it's hard for some of us spiritual types to want to keep our feet on the ground, because sometimes we feel judged or misunderstood by the less-awakened people around us. Just remember that if you ever want to create something in this world—a business, more impact, anything—you have to *be here*. Think of Scooby Doo: when he wants to run away, he jumps into the air and spins his paws around like crazy but doesn't get anywhere. *It's not until he hits the ground that he gains traction and starts moving.* Remember that the next time you'd prefer to float around in the ether but still live your calling.

Now, go have *fun!*

Its fun (not to mention fulfilling, rewarding, and inspiring to others) to live your brilliant, divinely-guided and inspired life! *Fun* is something the Keepers are always telling people to have more of. Don't take life, or your spiritual practice, too seriously. Life on Planet Earth is all about using the senses: seeing glorious things like sunsets, the faces of children, the sacred geometry in the petals of a flower, smelling the ocean or freshly-cut grass or a lime spraying out its juicy freshness. Enjoy your food, enjoy your body, enjoy sex, touching and being touched, running through the fields, laughing and shouting for joy. *You're here for a reason. Have fun while you live it.*

About the Author

Elizabeth Locey, Ph.D., is in the business of making other businesses soar.

As you've just read, Elizabeth left a successful academic career in 2010 to become a spiritual business coach and Akashic Reocrds consultant. Today, she empowers entrepreneurs + business leaders who are on a mission to make the world a better place, to create those shifts faster than you could ever imagine. As a clear channel, she'll help you to connect with the answers and tools you need to propel your business forward on a quantum level.

Elizabeth would love to hear from you about how you are using and learning from the principles she has outlined above and invites you to connect with her:

on Facebook http://facebook.com/ElizabethLocey,

on Twitter http://twitter.com/ElizabethLocey or

via email at elizabeth@elizabethlocey.com

Visit http://elizabethlocey.com to learn more about Elizabeth, the Akashic Records, how you might work together, or to listen to a live channeling of the Records on her blog where there are lots to choose from and more being added every month. This is also where you can pick up Elizabeth's free gift and subscribe to her newsletter if this speaks to you.

Cracking the Ceiling

Trish Carr

They call me the "Results Revolutionary" for a couple of reasons. One reason is that I achieve whatever I put my mind to and *I GET RESULTS*, and also help my clients get results and get results *now*, which often calls for revolutionary thinking.

Anytime I've ever had a single-minded focus to achieve something, I've achieved it. Whether it was moving up the corporate ladder, growing a phenomenal community with Women's Prosperity Network, or getting healthy and fit to the tune of shedding 110 pounds (and keeping it off), I achieve what I set out to achieve. I know that you do, too.

The origin of the moniker, and the second reason I'm called the "Results Revolutionary," is that when I was a teenager my sister, Susan Wiener, accurately coined me "rebel with a cause." I've always had some cause to fight for, spaying and neutering your pets, human rights, taking care of our planet and more. From deep within my core, I'm a revolutionary. I want to effect positive change. It's not what I do, *it's who I am* and I am the most alive when I'm making a difference. I can't tell you where my revolutionary spark started, but I can tell you when one issue ignited a passion that has been a life-long mission.

Growing up in the late 1960's and early 1970's I noticed that moms stayed home and dads went to work. My mom stayed home AND she worked. She did a variety of things; she sold Sarah Coventry costume jewelry, she sold Avon and she took in ironing. Every few days we'd go pick up laundry from the "rich" neighborhood. I'd hang out with her for hours as she ironed piece after piece, perfectly moistening them with her home-made sprinkler made out of one of those iconic green Coke bottles while I played dress up with the dozens of Avon lipstick samples and wide array of Sarah Coventry jewelry. Who knew she was ahead of her time, being in direct sales way before "Multi-Level Marketing" was ever heard of.

In the mid-60's my mom had to start working "outside the home" as they said in those days. I didn't know at the time that a separation and ultimately a divorce were in her future. Being a graduate of the prestigious Katherine Gibbs School, the premier secretarial school for women, she brushed up on her shorthand and typing and soon landed a job on Wall Street, the ultimate job. Despite juggling four school-aged children, an often unreliable husband, and a 90-minute commute, she was thrilled.

I didn't know at the time that this was a business climate where women were nowhere near being equal to men. Moms working outside the house were teachers, nurses, cashiers or secretaries. An Administrative Assistant? That was a secretary who couldn't type – usually a man – who was paid more than a secretary. There was a lot of that going around. Men were junior accountants and women were bookkeepers – same job, but a definite pay differential. In 1960, women were paid approximately 40 cents for every dollar a man earned.

My other female role models were nuns. In Catholic schools, the nuns were revered and most of us at one time or another wanted to be a nun when we grew up. At least I did, until I was about 12 and discovered boys!

So in high school it was clear I needed to learn shorthand and typing if I wanted to have a career. My mother's mantra, "As long as you can type, you'll always be able to take care of yourself." Again, she was ahead of her time as being able to type is pretty much a necessity in today's world.

My first job was with a family-owned business where there were two women, one was the owner's sister, Ruth, who did bookkeeping (and was paid as a bookkeeper, not a junior accountant). The other was the owner's wife, Dorothy, and I don't know exactly what she did other than fight with Ruth. Role models they weren't. I did invoicing and general clerical support. I hated it. Sitting at a typewriter all day, listening to constant squabbling and trying to make sense of the scribbled notes from the well-paid salesmen was tedious, boring and exasperating.

From there I held a series of administrative jobs until I got the *last job I'd ever have*, the Holy Grail, a job at the PHONE COMPANY (this is where the angels chime in). If you worked for the phone company you were set for life. Everyone who worked there retired from there. Or at least that's what we believed was true. And it probably was then - but not now. According to the Bureau of Labor Statistics, the average worker currently holds 10 different jobs before age 40, and this number is projected to grow. Forrester Research predicts that today's youngest workers will hold 12 to 15 jobs in their lifetime.

It was at the phone company that my revolutionary sparks were fueled and ignited. For the first time I saw what the real implication of junior accountant vs. bookkeeper meant. It meant that women were working as hard as or harder than men in similar jobs and being paid less. The male-dominated, technical jobs paid 30% more than the female-dominated customer service positions which required more knowledge and training and had sales quotas. Women who held both technical and administrative jobs said that the technical jobs were infinitely simpler and easier. And advancement for women was limited by the archaic thinking that mothers weren't able to take on any "real" responsibility at work.

The bookkeeper vs. junior accountant mentality also meant that women who did have the talent and persistence to land jobs in male dominated arenas were often treated unfairly by their male counterparts. In 1979 I met Margaret, an Account Executive, who was a highly regarded sales woman. Margaret had been an account executive for almost 20 years and for many of those early years was the only woman on the team. In the early days, Margaret would often come to work full of vim and vigor, ready to engage and serve her prospects and customers only to find her:

Leads list ruined with spilled coffee
Drawers filled with talcum powder
Files missing or half empty
Chair broken or dirty
Desk sticky and dirty from some foreign substance
Phone messages torn up and in the trash
And much more...

It was obvious she was not wanted there. She was clearly being bullied by the ultimate coward, the bully that doesn't show his face. Every time they tried to beat her down, she'd come back stronger, selling more products and getting more new clients. Despite the constant attempts to dampen her spirits, she became the team's leading sales person and went on to a long, successful career.

While we don't see that kind of overt discrimination today, women have still not reached economic equality. The Dalai Lama says, "The world will be saved by the western woman." I believe that is possible and infinitely more probable when we stand as equals on the economic playing field. Yes, there are many women who have made a powerful difference despite having the appearance of little or no economic power, Mother Theresa, Susan B. Anthony, Rosa Parks and others. Don't think for a moment though that these women achieved notoriety and made a global difference with no money. On the contrary, they were part of a team effort that included significant financial donations for the cause.

In 1978 women earned 64 cents for every dollar a man earned. According to the American Center for Progress' 2013 study, 25 years later that number has risen only 13 cents. Here's what the study shows:

"Though women form about half of the U.S. labor force, they get paid significantly less than men do. On average, a woman worker earns about 77 cents for every dollar that a white man is paid for an equivalent amount of work. The situation is a lot worse for women workers of color. On average, African American women earn 63 cents on the dollar, while Hispanic women earn just 54 cents for every dollar a man earns."

Women make up 49.6% of the world's population, and 50.6% of the U.S. population, yet the world's governments and religious systems are primarily ruled by men. We are making progress with more and more women in business, sports, government and in the media; however, we have a long way to go until we achieve economic equality. I am optimistic though. In my consulting business and in the organization I co-founded with my two sisters, Women's Prosperity Network, I see more and more women stepping up and claiming their power by pursuing lucrative careers and opening businesses.

According to the 2013 State of Women Owned Business Report by American Express, the number of women-owned businesses in the US has increased 59% since 1997 with 8.6 million women-owned companies generating more than $1.3 trillion in revenue and employing nearly 7.8 million people.

The numbers are going in the right direction and every day I see more and more committed, talented women opening businesses and doing what it takes to achieve success. And ladies, most importantly, we are doing it on OUR terms, achieving success as WE define it and achieving that success using the relationship building qualities we share as women. I am optimistic about our future, about our ability to effect positive change in our world. And I know somewhere up there my mother, Margaret and countless other women trailblazers are cheering us on.

About the Author

Trish Carr is a dynamic international speaker, author, executive business coach & leadership consultant with an expansive background in sales, marketing, customer service and peak performance training. Trish has shared the stage with some of the world's best-known speakers including Jack Canfield, Nancy Matthews, Bob Burg, Loral Langemeier, Steadman Graham and many more.

She is the author of "Sizzling Strategies for Success," a contributor to "Visionaries with Guts," and is co-founder of the Women's Prosperity Network (WPNGlobal.com), a global enterprise dedicated to inspiring, educating and empowering women and men within a trusted network of professionals.

As a consultant, coach and educator, Trish has worked with leaders and front-line employees in Fortune 500 companies, as well as with entrepreneurs and individuals.

If you'd like information on having Trish speak at your company or event or ordering her books or audio programs, please contact her at Revolutionary Consulting, Inc.

Trish@TrishCarr.com (954) 475-2178
www.TrishCarr.com

Setting Sail: Following Through on Your Aha Moment!

Lisa Caroglanian Dorazio

It takes approximately 20 to 40 nanoseconds of time for a fusion reaction in a hydrogen bomb. Not unlike the process of nuclear energy, when "two light atomic nuclei combine to form one," a past experience when combined with the reality of a future thought or action presents itself in the form of an **Aha Moment**. Though we experience many **Aha Moments** in our lifetime, the moment of inspiration that propels you to attain your future goals and dreams may be lost on you if you are not prepared to receive the rich gift of insight.

At one point in my life, in the not-so-distant past, I almost threw away the map to a treasure chest of jewels and the key that would unlock the buried loot. Are you the least bit curious to know how I found the lost key to such a treasure chest of wonder? If you have one of those inquiring minds and want answers to the whereabouts of these golden nuggets, be steadfast in your belief that you too can be the "Captain of your own Conviction" and champion for your cause. Being committed to an idea or belief is one thing; recognizing that you are destined to take action is when your sirens start to go off. Let me tell you about the moment in time when I realized my calling.

First, you will need to help me, Captain Lisa, pull up anchor and set sail over charted and not-so-charted seas of life. After agreeing to cast off and set sail on the ship of hope and promise, your journey to the land of lustrous longing will set you on a course to soul-feeding fertile ground. Like satisfying a growling stomach with a scrumptious meal, your cravings, once satisfied, will stimulate your hunger to do bigger and better things in the world.

My hope for you is that by gaining insight into my past, present and future you will discover who am I, what I have been through and where my ship will sail. Along the path you will learn about my encounters, my crew mates and more, about some of my passions. My dream, which I call "mothering many globally," evolved over time. There are scads of organizations – Amma, Big Brothers Big Sisters, and Mothers against Drunk Drivers, to name a few – that have the common thread of championing causes for children. The weaving of the cloth for my unique movement was born from the fibre of desire to help women and children. To understand the why of my intense desire to advocate for children you need to know who the voyager is.

Who am I? I was born in Washington, D.C. before John F. Kennedy was inaugurated President of the United States of America. My family was your typical nuclear family. I was blessed with great parents and an older brother. What might surprise you is that from infancy I knew I was special and that I was loved. Despite the rumblings from time to time that I was spoiled (didn't we all hear that as children), I learned from an early age that tough love was the best kind of love.

Tough love in our family meant that even at a young age you had responsibilities. You were expected to do chores and homework (to include getting high marks), respect your elders and be law abiding citizens. We volunteered to cut the church grass, shovel snow off the neighbors' sidewalks and driveways, and no, we did not do it for money, but rather for the simple act of kindness unto others. We were taught biblical morals and lived the *Golden Rule* principal that one should behave towards others as we would expect others to behave towards ourselves. Respect and honesty were given policies. We were told to go play in traffic – not literally, but figuratively – knowing full well that our parents did not want us to be harmed. Instilled in us was the core belief that our parents loved us but there was a time and place for everything. We knew those words were much the same as the policy of being seen and not heard when company was present. In other words, we were given the freedom as children to be children while the adults were left to whatever adults did in their work and play time. All the while our parents, and community at-large, reinforced their love, support and devotion to us.

My parents were first generation children of immigrant parents who survived the 1915 genocide of the Armenian people. They had no choice but to leave their homeland for lands and languages unknown. My dad's parents landed in Canada, eventually making their way across the 49th parallel to Washington, D.C., while my mother's parents and grandparents came ashore, like the pilgrims, to the Commonwealth of Massachusetts. Their lives were not easy, but family and long days of hard work saw them through the tough times. There was always a "can do" attitude which transcended through the generations to a "glass is half full" philosophy towards life. They volunteered in their communities and passed on their strong belief systems down through the years.

As we know today, our belief systems are formed at a very early age. They are like eye glasses. Depending on your prescription, your vision might be crystal clear or blurry, blocking the truth. I wore rose-colored glasses, seeing no roadblocks to my success and happiness. I believed I could do anything I set my mind to do. I am a lucky lady, though, as my parents rarely discouraged me from trying something new. It is not by coincidence that I was also conditioned to believe that everything happens for a reason; God has a plan. As a Christian you are taught to believe unconditionally that God's Plan is the perfect plan. You do not apply logic to those conscious and subconscious thoughts, but simply accept the hands you are dealt. However, children grow up and challenge belief systems repeatedly until they are proven right or wrong. I was no different.

My 20s and early 30s were pretty typical. I graduated from university, worked, volunteered, hung out with my friends and family. I traveled every chance I had, enjoying life to the fullest. Until the point at which I met and married my husband, I was convinced that my mission in life was to serve my alma mater, my church, family and friends. I thought I would always live in the home I bought near my parents, looking after them as they aged. Did I know the tides had turned? Lo and behold the ebb and flow had changed. It was time to hoist those new sails. Ahoy!

In the third decade of my life I met and married my husband Dan. Unlike the predictability of tide tables, being married to an NCAA football coach assures you of one thing – your residential anchor will not be dropped for long. We have been so fortunate in the last 17 years to have lived in Bowie, Maryland; Watertown, Massachusetts; Calgary, Alberta; and Abbotsford, British Columbia. As I said *I am lucky* and yes, in the first couple of years of my married life I experienced all of the best and worst the coaching world could offer. We lived apart, together, in different states and in different countries. Yes, we moved many times. We moved ourselves five times in the first two years of marriage. We got pregnant time and time again but sadly, the babies died. While I never had the limiting belief that my life role would be that of Jane Wyatt as Margaret Anderson in *Father Knows Best,* raising children and retiring in the same home, I had not planned on the troublesome life of Lucy Ricardo. At least she had one child of her own in Little Ricky.

I was grateful for all that I had, but the reality of raising children for me morphed into a non-conventional definition of child rearing. After experiencing the agonizing loss of children, I affirm to you that *I am lucky* to have grown, gained strength, come into my greater purpose and, most importantly, have the power of sight to recognize why I exist. I pondered the blessings of my "Starbucks Starlets," a group of former coffee shop co-workers who adopted me as their BC Mom. Because of their encouragement and support of my other friends and family, I know that I am a difference maker. You are too! I encourage you, if you have not already, to invite greatness into your life.

Like learning to tie a sailor's knot, there are steps one must take on the journey towards greatness. While some may tack back and forth to their final destination, my advice to you would be to learn from my experiences and approach your journey in a direct manner, but always stay in motion.

Get over yourself and out of your own way! If you have found that you have gotten too full of your egocentric self, then it is time to be humbled. Examine your thoughts, goals and actions, and jump on board with the vital role that the universal theatre affords you by taking extreme action. You will find the sun will rise and set on your gifts and talents as it has on mine. I love to interact with people and I love to empower individuals to follow their passions. It was only after years of self discovery that I changed my course of action. It was through networking, education and acquiring certain skills that I uncovered the answers to how I would go forward with the venture of my heart. What tugs at your heart strings will be uncovered if you start now, asking yourself daily, what you can do to move yourself forward towards accomplishing your goals. Always display an attitude of gratitude by practicing daily positive affirmations. Be mentally tough like *The Little Engine That Could* by implementing a system that will help you succeed in fulfilling all that you desire.

The following simple steps, when practiced consistently, will steer you and your rudders forward to reach your goals:

Set your compass
Define inspirational goals
Create a challenging visual working plan
Ask for guidance
Maintain your course
Identify and adjust your strengths and weaknesses
Perform daily check-ups of your belief system
Volunteer
Look beyond the horizon
Have contingency plans
Initiate joint ventures
Revisit your goals

Being realistic when establishing your goals is not always required. Why shouldn't you be relentless and fearless in establishing your goals? Realistically you can expect a percentage of "Negative Nellies" who will attempt to annoyingly distract you from your focus. Great stamina will be required of you to avoid these dysfunctional groups of people who will vigorously attempt to pirate your very noble efforts. Always have a positive, proactive crew of people on your ship's deck. Always focus on the front of your boat, only looking aft as a point of reference in reassessing your goals, timelines, strengths and weaknesses.

Push yourself regularly to get out and interact with a myriad of positive, proactive people. I am fortunate to have a network of assertive individuals who will not hesitate to respectfully offer a difference of opinion. This has allowed me to stretch myself beyond a traditional support system. I encourage you to think outside the box and seek and discover opportunities to join mastermind groups.

As you learned earlier in this chapter, I come from a family who strongly believes in service to community. Every coin has two sides. If you toss the "volunteer coin" you will find the flip side of giving is that you gain so much joy from the act of giving. You also naturally build another network of individuals that you can go to for advice. When you earnestly employ the consistent practice of being grateful, people will come out of the woodwork to help you. Believe this and you will achieve your desired results!

As it would take many more pages that are available to delve into a more in-depth analysis of who I am, what I have done in my lifetime, how I am going to accomplish all that I foresee in the future and who will be part of my sailing crew on the boat to fulfilling my charitable contributions, I would like to conclude our short time together here by sharing with you the why of my cause? I discovered through my association with the founder and CEO of SendOutCards®, Kody Bateman, that you need to dig down really deep and scope out the "why that makes you want to cry."

I believe God and the Universe put people, places and things in your path to catapult you to the moon and stars above. I am a Cancer, a "Moon Child." I am drawn to water and believe that you can wash away negativity and replace it with positive forces in your life. I believe that tragedy is to comedy as tragedy is to blessing. With every intention to be redundant, I would like to emphasize that the why's that make me want to cry were born from tragedies.

The first reason for wanting to raise funds and awareness of the needs of sick children and orphans began at a very tender age. Wanting a younger sibling may have been a contributing factor, but clearly my brother's accident in which he lost eyesight motivated my strong desire to contribute to children's hospitals. To this day those childhood experiences conjure up emotions that make me cry. Later, I used to say as a single unmarried woman that if I didn't get married I would want to adopt a child. After losing my child, the gravity of this incident forced all those emotions to the surface. Clearly an incident of this magnitude in any family would make an indelible impression.

My second reason was due to the lifelong influence of my maternal Grandfather Vahram Der Parseghian. He was quite the drama king, a trained Shakespearean actor, but there was no drama, just pure heartache when he recounted stories of his life. You see, when my Grandfather Vahram was just a 14-

year-old boy he could no longer care for his parentless siblings. He was forced, amidst outbreaks of cholera, typhoid and lice, to take his brother and sister by the hand and deposit them into Holy Etchmiadzin, the Mother Church of all Armenians. My Grandfather told us of the woes of his siblings being separated from one another. His brother was shipped off to Egypt while his sister was sent to Syria. He continued to send money for their care despite losing touch. Fifteen years later he was miraculously reunited with his sister and 35 years later with his brother.

Since my initial **Aha Moment**, in which I acknowledged my intention to raise funds and awareness for children and their families, I have had seismic **Aha Moments**. One of the most historic moments came when I visited Armenia and walked in the steps of my forefathers. It was then that I realized the power in my mission. Walking the grounds of Holy Etchmiadzin and visiting *Our Lady of Armenia Center* in Gyumri, Armenia, validated my calling.

I believe that I had a subconscious intention to honor Christina Dorazio, the daughter my husband and I lost in 1999. Even though I knew that I wanted to create a legacy to honor all my relatives, dead and alive, I could not have known the depths to which I could reach toward that end. Had it not been for my willingness to put myself out there in the world and attend the *2010 Making a Difference* SendOutCards® convention, I might still be thinking about my plans instead of having the guts to act on my dreams.

What are your goals? My journey includes raising awareness and funds for children through donations to children's hospitals and orphanages globally.

What is your dream? My vision is to have a free-flowing supply of funds to designated charities.

What is the "why that makes you cry?" You already know the reasons for my why.

Do not leave until tomorrow what you can do today. Begin those conversations that will spearhead you towards your targets. Be a difference maker in the world. Ignore the naysayers and draw on your successes to reach out to others.

Be vigilant and steadfast in your focus on the limitless positive people and energies in the universe. As the sun rises each and every day, so too will you be prepared for your **Aha Moment**.

Remember the words of the ancient Chinese philosopher Laozi, *"A journey of a thousand miles begins with a single step."* I look forward to the christening of your ship. Bon voyage!

About the Author

Lisa Caroglanian Dorazio, Founder and CEO of CanAmeri Consulting, Inc. and owner of a greeting card/gifting business, assists professionals with the administrative and marketing aspects of their commercial enterprises. With 40+ years in business, Lisa honed her skills in sales, human resources, marketing and management. Her education and experience, coupled with her passion for writing, now enable her to serve the global community by connecting consumers and entrepreneurs through innovative communication strategies.

Lisa is a soon-to-be-published author of a book detailing her trial of losing a child through miscarriage, which she hopes will help other women and families contending with a similar loss. Lisa's desire to serve the larger community is reflected in her vision to assist children's hospitals and orphanages. With loyalty and gratitude, and through sharing her life motto "Fly Like an Eagle", Lisa helps family, friends and colleagues empower themselves to enhance our world.

Contact Lisa Caroglanian Dorazio:
www.canamericonsulting.com
www.sendoutcards.com/dorazio
info@canamericonsulting.com
604-859-3977 (Canada)
301-717-2104 (USA)
Facebook: CanAmeri Consulting, Inc.
Twitter: Lisa C. Dorazio@CanAmeriConsult
LinkedIn: Lisa Caroglanian Dorazio
Skype: Canamericonsulting
Klout: Lisa Dorazio

Lock the Door - Unlock the Possibilities

Marcella Scherer

Locked out? What do you mean locked out and out of business? Are you kidding me? My livelihood depends on this business! How dare you send a locksmith to close the showroom after I helped you build your business from the ground up! What about all my hard work, overtime and commuting 85 miles each way to work? You made a promise!

All I can say is I didn't see it coming! I feel like I just got the rug pulled out from underneath me! I'm angry, I'm resentful. With no job, no financial resources or local family to fall back on, what's a girl gonna do?

On that cloudy day in July of 1990, at the age of 27, I had just experienced one of the worst days of my life. With nowhere to turn, I had to clear my head and do something fast! My boss, and business owner of the wholesale women's apparel business I had worked my hinny off for, for 2 ½ years in Atlanta, Georgia was now closing up shop. My dream job was officially gone with the change of a lock. My dream of breaking through the glass ceiling in the fashion industry was now locked in the showroom, behind the bolted door. I resented the fact that I had worked so hard to expand his business and build his company, and now I had nothing to show for it.

Today, in hindsight, it was probably the BEST day of my life. It was on that day that I officially became an entrepreneur, truly, out of necessity, not by choice. When the going got tough, I found out what I was made of. I discovered my core values and looked at what was important in my life. It was the first of three pivotal conversations that propelled me in my journey to becoming the person I am today. Now, after 25 years of entrepreneurship, a successful marriage of 20 years and as a million dollar earner in my industry, I can say it was the key that unlocked my future.

I needed to act quickly, as I had major bills due in three weeks. How could I earn some fast cash while I searched for a new job? Wait, I did have something in my "back pocket"! I had my certification as an image consultant from a year earlier. I had taken a course to learn about what colors to wear for your skin tone, makeup application and what clothes to wear for your body shape. At the time, I thought it would be useful information that could help me in my industry. Besides, I was curious how it all worked. I figured at the very least, the course would help me look and feel better about myself. I had invested $1500 at the time and had set what I had learned aside; not taking action, because of life's other distractions.

Maybe this was my time. Perhaps I had the perfect opportunity right in my lap and wasn't even aware. I needed to take a second look at this as a serious option; as my "Plan B." What were my alternatives? I was so burnt out, deflated and emotionally drained after all that was happening.

Should I go work for someone else and have the carpet potentially yanked out from underneath me again? Or would I build something for someone else rather than get credit and earn the money for myself? I wanted flexibility and the last thing I wanted was another job that would take me down the same road. I also needed flexibility because I was in a relationship with a wonderful man who was about to move away after 10 months of dating. He had just graduated from chiropractic school and had high hopes of building his own practice in South Florida. We were building a relationship that would last. We had plans of a future together.

The momentum for change and new possibilities all started with "the call" I got from one of my previous company's competitors. They asked me to come in for an interview. A new career was the last thing I wanted, but a girl's got to do what a girl's got to do. My girlfriend gave me some very valuable advice from her commercial real estate experience. She suggested I go in and ask for everything I really wanted or would be willing to do before I would even consider working for someone else. It caused a shift in my thinking. I had promised myself I would not go down the same road again and set myself up to get stuck in a job I didn't want in the first place.

So I came up with a list. Here is what it looked like:

- Work 4 days instead of 5, a total of 28 hours a week, leaving at 4:30 instead of 5:30
- Have flexibility to take off when I wanted to head to Florida to see my boyfriend with no questions asked
- To have full time benefits and full time pay for my 28 hour week with generous commissions when I brought in new clients or big orders
- To go on buying trips to NY and have input and say on clothing that would suit my client's needs
- To have my travel expenses paid when I needed to visit my client's boutiques in various cities

What the heck, I had nothing to lose! I was so frazzled that I didn't really care if I got the job or not after my last experience. I figured if I would ask for the moon, the stars and the sky, even if I made it to the moon, I would be satisfied, able to pay my bills, see my boyfriend and work on my image consulting business.

Guess what? THEY GAVE ME WHAT I ASKED FOR!!! I COULDN'T EVEN BELIEVE IT! IT ALL STARTED WITH A CONVERSATION AND BEING CLEAR ON WHAT IT WAS THAT I WANTED. WOW!

As I look back at that time of my life, I realize that there are a few things that I have discovered that are key to moving on after the unexpected.

Key #1 ... Always be open to the possibilities of having new conversations and get clear on what you want.

Over the course of the next 14 months, I continued to plug along, working my new job in Atlanta, building my image consulting business and dating my boyfriend, Mark, long distance in South Florida. When Mark passed the chiropractic board exams, we decided it was time for me to move. We both had no money. To continue our long distance romance was a huge financial burden, not to mention a strain on our relationship. Mark was forced to live with his parents while he completed his mandatory internship earning $200 per week. Moving in with him was not an option. Therefore, supporting myself was essential to my move.

I let my heart lead the way. I rented a U-Haul and my girlfriend and I headed south leaving behind everything that had been familiar and comfortable for the last 6 years. My friends, my livelihood and my image business were all in the rear view mirror as I drove toward my new life. With a whopping $3700 to my name, no job or a place to live, I remember crying most of the drive down and asking myself "what the heck am I doing?" My friends thought I was crazy for not getting engaged before I went, but I just knew that I had to live in the same town as Mark before I could consider the proposition of getting married. To me, the thought of that commitment was scarier than the move!

Far out of my comfort zone, I was determined to figure things out and find a way. I knew four people; Mark, his parents and an acquaintance from Atlanta. My only hope that this would work came from being close to the love of my life. I was scared. How was I going to make it in a new city with no money, no contacts and no job? I was afraid. I cried myself to sleep at night. I was unsure and filled with self-doubt not knowing what the future held for me. I relied on the power of positive thoughts and prayers. I wrote affirmations in my journal. I read powerful books, said prayers and had conversations with myself to keep a positive attitude and everything in perspective.

My prayers were answered when I asked around and found a girl looking for a roommate in an apartment close to the beach. I felt it was meant to be! While moving in to my new apartment, I went through most of my cash. Now the pressure was really on. If I wanted to continue to work in the fashion industry, which was familiar, I would have had to travel 1 ½ hours back and forth to Miami. Been there done that. The other option was to take a BIG step backwards and settle by working in retail being paid significantly less with crazy hours. I was not going down that road again, literally! At least I had learned something, right?

Mark was on the same path as I was. His living at home with his parents was not ideal, either. Going on a date meant finding something to do for free. Instead of going out to eat, we usually would raid his mother's pantry. Something new to wear had to come from a consignment store or thrift shop. Even though we had no money, we forged ahead. It was Mark who encouraged me to follow my passion for having my own business to help women look their best with wardrobe, makeup and skincare. He always offered reassurance by telling me to keep moving forward. When I was discouraged or challenged, he would draw a big arrow with a black magic marker on a post it note that I would put in a prominent place as a reminder to stay focused on my dream. Despite the circumstances, we were both determined to move toward the bigger picture of living our dream life together, having our own businesses and helping others.

Then, out of the blue, I met a woman who lived in a high end community who was looking for an aerobics instructor. After my many years studying as a ballet dancer and teaching aerobics in Atlanta, I figured it might be a great way to make some cash for groceries and gas. This totally unforeseen opportunity was a gift from God; I know it! They paid me $450/week teaching just three 1 hour classes!!! Are you kidding? The universe provided and now I could breathe! With at least enough to make ends meet, I could focus on doing what I loved and forge ahead to get things going with my image consulting business.

Mark invited me to go to a Chamber of Commerce meeting with him to network and get a pulse of what was happening in the community. I had never done that, but what did I have to lose?

You might have guessed that because of my passion for fashion and working on the wholesale side of the industry, I had some pretty killer clothes. Knowing what to look for, I even found great clothes in consignment shops. What I quickly discovered was that the clothing people wore in South Florida, compared to those in Atlanta was like night and day. Truly, I was aghast at what people were showing up in to a networking meeting! And to think they were there to promote their businesses! I was like... really??? I quickly figured out that there was an opportunity here, and a great need for what I offered. I just had NO idea how it was going to happen, but I did know that failure was NOT an option.

Key #2... Always look the part. You never know who you will meet.

Have you ever been caught off guard running into someone when you are not looking your best; no makeup, bad hair and in your "hanging out" clothes? All I can say, is I am so grateful I was looking "the part" that day, because it just so happened that I ran into a salon owner I had met at the Chamber meeting. We ended up having a conversation, right in the grocery store that lead to me renting a space in her salon to do makeovers and color analysis. It was a great proposition. Even though I had to pay money for the space, I jumped on it. I soon discovered that I was going to have to be responsible for bringing in my own clients if I wanted to make money. Hanging out with no pay, hoping to convert other employee's clients to my own was not a good solution. I needed to muster up some confidence and be BOLD. I noticed they listed all the different organizations and local meetings in the newspaper every Monday. I thought if I could get in front of women's groups, I could meet new connections and get new business.

So, I started dialing for dollars. I would take a deep breath with my prepared script and hope for the best, not always knowing what I was going to say or how the conversation would work out. I called them, gave my 30 second commercial and then asked if they were looking for guest speakers. Jackpot! I got some bookings, a few people said "no, not now" and others said they would get back to me.

Now I was PETRIFIED!! I had never spoken in front of more than 4 people at a time! I purchased a presentation and script to prepare my talk. Shaking and feeling as though I would throw up any second, I read the script with a flashlight, from behind the projector during my 1st presentation. I was over the hurdle! Whew! They loved what I shared and I even got a few new clients! I was excited! I pressed on; continuing to practice and get in front of new groups. I had a few lucky breaks for my persistence and tenacity. I landed a gig with Florida Power and Light to do "Image Update Workshops" for their employees. It was the first time I had ever written a big contract and negotiated it to get paid for speaking. I heard my girlfriend saying in my head, "Ask for what it is that you want". So I did..., and I got the gig for multiple workshops at various campus locations. They even paid me the fee that I asked!

That one contract multiplied and exploded my business exponentially. It all started with "The One", as we say in WPN. The ONE was the HR Director who said "yes" to my programs and helped me to propel my business and connections to a whole new level.

Key #3... Do what scares you the most and take risks!

I have learned so much about myself from my life's journey. Through this process I have discovered my purpose. It is now my passion to help other women, not only to look and feel their best from head to toe, but to also build their confidence and belief from the inside out. Coaching others to be empowered from within, to have their own success and achievements helped me to realize my own dreams.

There were so many people along the way who encouraged and coached me so that I could expand my mind, my horizons and create possibilities I had never imagined. Now I have the opportunity to empower others in the same way. I would not be the leader that I am today had I not had the chance to share my own transformational journey; with others and grow alongside of them. Each person who I have had the honor of working with has their own unique style, personality and vision. It thrills me that I can see the beauty and individuality of each of them; just like a flower in a beautiful bouquet unfolding in bloom. It is amazing what a little lipstick and wearing the right clothes, in the best colors for her, will do for a woman. It blends her inner and outer beauty, allowing her to stand in the greatness of who she is with confidence and authenticity.

Whether you work for yourself or someone else, always have additional streams of income so not all your eggs are in one basket. Have that Plan B, keeping in mind that it should have something to do with your passions in life.

In hindsight, I am very grateful for all my struggles, obstacles and challenges that have happened over the years. I am grateful for the doors being locked and for having nowhere to turn but within. Through it all, I discovered that I had everything I needed all along. I'm grateful for the amazing conversations and opportunities I was open to having along the way. I know that you can achieve anything that you set your mind to. With a little lipstick, lol, courage and lots of perseverance, you can unlock the keys to your heart, your life and your future.

"Nothing is impossible, the word itself says 'I'm possible'!"
~Audrey Hepburn

About the Author

Marcella Scherer is passionate about helping others to shine from the inside out! As a certified image consultant, trainer and seasoned entrepreneur, her expertise is in fashion, makeup, skincare, and developing leaders.

Marcella works with clients ranging from today's "average" women to national celebrities, customizing their look using color analysis, personal shopping and wardrobe services. Along with Image consulting, Mrs. Scherer with her national team is in the top 1% of BeautiControl, her affiliate skincare and cosmetic company. She is a national speaker and has also been featured in Palm Beach Post, Kiplingers Report, ESPN and local TV stations.

Serving on various boards of nonprofit organizations, Marcella has a true passion for making a difference and bringing out the best in others.

Contact her at 561-743-5945
marcella@marcellascherer.com
or www.marcellascherer.com

The Power of Community

Sue Townsend

My destiny as an entrepreneur was set at a very young age. My grand uncle was Tom Carvel, founder of the Carvel ice cream franchise chain. Through him, I had a taste of the "good life" that comes with being a successful, wealthy, business owner, and I liked it!

I've had numerous business ventures. My parents, grandmother, aunts, and uncles were all incredibly supportive through my many endeavors, and they became sounding boards for my business ideas. I received a lot of advice from them, sometimes welcome, sometimes not, and while I didn't realize it at the time, I was completely dependent on them, and they were the pillars of my success. They were my Community. I often thought about what I would have done if I hadn't had this Community. Would I have had the confidence to take such financial risks if I hadn't had a family behind me to catch me if I failed? Would I have had the courage to go out on my own and start my own businesses if I didn't have an uncle like Tom Carvel telling me that with hard work I could do anything and be a success? Probably not. I needed their approval and that's what gave me the confidence to move forward. Without the support of my Community, I most definitely would have played it safe and gotten a 9 to 5 job and lived happily, though probably not fulfilled, ever after.

My most consistent business has been real estate. Uncle

Tom sponsored me in getting my real estate salesperson's license at the age of 24. As soon as I was eligible, I applied for and received my broker's license. I have been in the real estate business for my entire working life and currently I am a real estate broker and investor. That's how I pay the bills, but my real passion is inventing. I dreamed up my first invention when I was 24 years old when I wallpapered the bathroom of my New York City condo. The idea was for a "wallpaper paster," and as I would end up doing dozens of times forward, I announced my great idea at a family dinner. My Community wasn't as intrigued with my idea as I was, but they were supportive all the same. It was then that Uncle Tom gave me a lesson on how to do a patent search, and the next business day I was on my way to the patent library in Manhattan.

I see most things in life from a business perspective, and I often have a new business idea or invention in the back of my mind. I tend to be a very academic person, and I study and research anything that piques my interest. I take business classes and attend seminars often, and I rarely read magazines unless they are business or golf-related. If I read a book, it's either business-related or biographical. I taught myself how to complete a patent application and saved myself thousands of dollars by circumventing the use of a patent attorney.

If I see a problem or a need for a product or service, my mind starts going into invention mode. I invented a golf cart seat cover because sitting on vinyl golf cart seats was hot, sticky and unsanitary. Now I have a business - Nif Tee Seat - selling golf cart seat covers. The list goes on and on. I have always been very independent and never believed that partnerships were for me, but when I needed advice or had business questions; I turned to my Community for guidance

Recently, I found myself unfulfilled with my current businesses. It was as though I were living a Monopoly game that had gone on too long. I needed a change. My father had passed away a few months prior to this, and he was the last one left of my Community. I found myself all alone, without the comfort of an elder family member to bounce ideas off of and to assure me that I was making good decisions. My life was in limbo, and I was desperately seeking a new direction. Luckily for me, I ended up getting involved in women's networking groups, and through them, my life and business began moving in that new direction.

In a very round-about way, completely by accident, I became very involved in women's networking groups. An author friend of mine asked me to go to a women's networking luncheon at which she was speaking. A few months later I got an email from the woman who organized that networking luncheon, inviting me to an event for women entrepreneurs. I went to the event and from the time I got there, I doubted my decision to be there. There were so many women there, and I only knew one of them. We sat a big round tables, and when the event started they cranked up music and said, "OK, now let's all start by hugging as many people in the room as you can!" I couldn't believe it! This was SO not me. I was WAY out of my comfort zone. I looked for the door and thought about making a quick exit, but I would have to pass by the woman who sent me the invitation if I left and I didn't want to insult her. So, I stayed for the event and even signed up for a course which altered the path of my business life.

The course, Personal Branding, was on-line, once a week, for 6 weeks. During the course, the trainer kept talking about how women have to support each other and work together. She kept saying that all the women in this class are each other's customers. My businesses are real estate and golf cart seat covers. I wasn't sure how many of these women were golfers and probably only a few may buy and sell real estate in the near future, so I really didn't see how these people were going to be my customers. The course made me realize that I needed to have a business or service that would serve all of these women.

Through this branding course, one woman kept talking about a group she goes to called Women's Prosperity Network. I decided to go to one of their meetings, and I figured since they met at Ruth's Chris Steakhouse, at the very least I'd have a good lunch! That meeting was nothing short of amazing. The women are all so positive and uplifting, and genuinely care about each other. I don't like to call WPN a networking group because it's so much more. After my first luncheon with them, I signed up. I have found my new community!

Along the way, I joined more groups. Invitations for get-togethers and meetings were coming at me so fast that I ended up missing events that I really wanted to attend. Then there was the problem of remembering who I had met at which event and what business they were in. I had business cards in all my handbags and all over my house and car. I couldn't remember who was who even with the cards. I needed a computer person, and I knew that I had met one at one of the get-togethers, but I couldn't remember the person's name. The result was a missed opportunity for both of us, because I hired someone I didn't know and the person I had met missed out on a job. I kept asking around if there was a directory for any of the groups, which there wasn't. That was my big "light bulb" moment: a women's referral directory was needed to serve the women I was meeting at these networking events. So, my latest venture is called the Women's Referral Directory. It's a centralized hub where women entrepreneurs can list themselves and their businesses or services, and participate in the interactive calendar. It acts as a centralized hub where women (and men, if they so choose!) can search for goods and services so that we can support each other. The Directory is global, and we have listings in the United States, Canada, and Jamaica. Thanks to my new community, I am back on track!

The importance of Community is apparent in all aspects of our lives. Especially in business, it is important to assemble an effective Community composed of trusted advisors and enthusiastic cheerleaders. The main principles of Community are grounded in the A-B-C-D's:

ACCOUNTIBILITY: From the time we are kids, when we are held accountable for our actions, the rewards are bigger. It's really no different in later life or in business. For example, I have an awesome personal trainer. Every night I complete a journal on her app of what I ate that day. I made a commitment not to drink wine for eight weeks, which is a very difficult commitment to keep, because I REALLY love wine! Since I have to be accountable to my trainer by completing my journal, it is very difficult to break my commitment. If you exchange ideas with your Community, personally or professionally, you are making a commitment to them to carry out those ideas, and the next time you meet, you will be held accountable. It's much easier to succeed when you have to be accountable to your Community than when you're trying to go it alone.

BELIEVE: You must believe in yourself and believe that you can succeed! When I was just a little girl, Uncle Tom told me to get the word CAN'T out of my vocabulary. If I slipped and used the word, in any context, he would scream, "Don't use that word", and he'd go into his entire explanation of why I was not permitted to ever use that word! It may sound crazy, but I urge you to take CAN'T out of your vocabulary and see what a difference it makes in your life. You CAN do anything! You have to believe in yourself in order to project your ideas effectively.

CHOICE: My sister-in-law planted the seed in my mind a long time ago that everything in life is a choice. One of the most important choices that you can make is who you spend your time with. We are all constantly learning, and we learn from other people. I want to be surrounded by positive, uplifting, like-minded people. I attend conferences, seminars, meetings and get-togethers because I am inspired by the women I meet at them. Listening to other women's stories about their lives and businesses motivates me to continue to excel in my business and my life. It is also important to be with people who are excited about your business, people who will help promote you and the business.

DUTY: As a member of your Community, you have a duty

to help other entrepreneurs as others have helped you. I especially love helping and inspiring young people to be creative and develop business ideas. Mentoring is very powerful both for you and the person you are mentoring. One of my proudest moments was when my nephew, then about 10 years old, asked me to help him think of an invention for an invention fair his school was having. I saw that as validation as an inventor. I am also going to be working on a project with my 16-year-old niece to get her involved in a business venture.

I was very lucky to have grown up in the family I did. The business influence I had from a very early age set a path to where I am today. I'm a single mother to my daughter Alex, whom I adopted from China when she was 20 months old. I'm trying to be the same positive influence on her, teaching her that she can do anything she wants to do. She is business minded and often gives me advice!

The bottom line is, as important as business and success are; it's much sweeter when it is recognized by people who matter. Make sure that your Community matters. They will be your strength when times are challenging and they will be your cheerleaders when times are good!

About the Author

Sue Townsend is the developer of the Women's Referral Directory, which is quickly becoming the "Angie's List" for women entrepreneurs. The Directory is a centralized hub where women (and men if they so choose), can list their products and services in a searchable directory. It's a growing, global directory, with listings in the United States, Canada and Jamaica.

Sue is an entrepreneur, inventor, real estate broker and investor. She is the inventor of Nif Tee Seat, the golf cart seat cover and also owns the real estate brokerage business, E Property Solution.

Sue is a single mom to 9 year old Alex, whom she adopted from China. They live in Boca Raton, FL. with their 3 dogs, Rosie, Oreo and Lily.

Contact Sue Townsend:

Townsue@aol.com

561-703-7594

www.WomensReferralDirectory.com

www.NifTeeSeat.com

www.SueTownsend.com

I Am Woman -- Hear Me Roar

Dr. Marla Friedman

The chrome coffee table, macramé plant holder and the wine bottle with years of accumulated candle wax is the decor in our living room. Helen Reddy's voice is belting out "I am Woman, Hear me Roar". Mom is wearing her favorite bellbottoms and singing along as she works in our brown and yellow kitchen. It's 1978.

Growing up in the 1970's, I experienced a time of women's lib and equality. Marlo Thomas's album *Free to Be You & Me* became a bestseller and a favorite record in our house. This children's album and subsequent film, explained to a new generation that boys could be nurses and girls could be doctors.

My mother wanted the best of both worlds: the ability to stay home with her children and also have a business. My parents were living in New York and then, with a transfer to Florida, where I was born, my mother sold pool chemicals and patio furniture, carrying her baby along. When I was two years old, we moved to Connecticut, where my mom began selling costume jewelry for a multi-level marking company. Her next venture led to bright yellow magnetic signs on our blue 1981 Volvo station wagon that read "The Handy Housewife." My mom had a carpentry and repair business in our small Connecticut town. How does a suburban mom become a carpenter? I have no idea.

One day she told us she was going away for 2 weeks to the Berkshires. She was going to learn how to build a home from scratch. Our father drove us to visit where we met her new friends in a wooded cabin. They resembled left-over hippies, drinking herbal tea and carrying hammers. My mom returned home with a desire for wood working and her own *Shopsmith* brand saw. It was inevitable that an impressionable young girl would catch the entrepreneurial spirit.

The Handy Housewife was so successful that clients began asking for window treatments, wallpaper and furniture. The natural next step on the path was for her to become an interior decorator. So, *Affordable Interiors* was born and it lived for many years. At age 12, I was attending trade shows, shopping at the Design Center in New York City and going to client appointments. My mother was invited to a new networking group which only permitted one person per profession to join. She jumped at the chance and the networking group proved to be beneficial to her decorating business. Mom enjoyed the group so much that she was one of the first to purchase a franchise. Over twenty years later, my mom continues to run the Connecticut Business Network International (BNI) Franchise. She has over 2,000 members and is still growing.

This desire for entrepreneurship seems natural for some people. My mother chose this path so she could be home with her children after school, unlike her own mother. She had a difficult childhood and wanted the opposite for her own children. My younger brother and I grew up with a mother who was highly involved in our lives. She was my Girl Scout Troop Leader and even took our troop to

Washington DC where her green whistle controlled a bus filled with 5th grade girls.

When it was time for summer camp, my mother applied to be the Arts & Crafts director at our local day camp so we could go together every day. My father traveled the Northeast for his job Monday-Friday, so my mom was always in charge. I don't think raising two kids in the suburbs was always easy.

My parents taught us independence and equality. Since my brother wasn't interested, my father taught me to change the oil in a car and took me to car races that his company sponsored. My mom enrolled us in extracurricular classes at a young age such as Spanish, typing, MS-DOS computer programming and violin lessons.

When I was 15, my parents allowed me to participate in a student exchange program in Spain. This experience had a huge impact on my life. It changed my perception of the world. The exposure to other cultures eventually led to my living in Belgium for 2 years for graduate school. While I was in high school, we hosted two exchange students in our home. My parents always exposed us to different cultural experiences such as attending jazz concerts, the ballet, Broadway musicals and museums in New York City. I remember being about 8 years old and going to an Ella Fitzgerald concert... and... I liked it. My brother apparently did too, because his life's work is focused on music.

In the early 90's my mother took me to Stephen Covey's all-day seminar. He spoke about his new book: *The Seven Habits of Highly Effective People*. This sparked my life-long interest in motivational seminars and the self-help industry.

My parents were always supportive and encouraged my brother and me to follow our dreams. I attended the

University of New Mexico to become an architect, even though there were few females in the profession at that time.

We drove our trusty Volvo cross-county, packed with my belongings. The day we arrived on campus and moved into my dorm, my mother took me to the University's career center. She looked at the board and told me to choose a work-study job. This clearly was not up for discussion. I applied to work at the Theater Department building sets. The job was tough, requiring every student to wear jeans in over 100 degree heat and use welding equipment in the shop. Sometimes we painted sets or climbed the 60 foot high grid over the stage. The middle-age theater director had a propensity for freshman girls and a complaint was launched which, thankfully, ended that job.

My next student job was counting bones in the University's Museum of Anthropology. One night, I was organizing the exhibits and was mistakenly locked in the museum with the lights turned off for the night. Frustrated with work study jobs, I ventured off campus for my next job and worked at the front desk of a national hotel chain.

The summer after my freshman year, I drove the Volvo cross country back to Connecticut. I should have known what was coming - a summer job. My friends would drive by in their convertibles on their way to the beach and wave as I was cutting grass and shoveling bark mulch on Main Street. Of course my mother had arranged this job for me with a female-owned landscaping business in town. When I returned to college in Albuquerque, I began selling cellular phones (the Motorola brick phone) and collaborated with my mother to open the first BNI chapter in New Mexico. She purchased the franchise and I launched and ran chapters which are still in existence. At 19 years old, I left my sorority house, where I lived, at 6 in the morning with my briefcase to run a BNI meeting and then head back to campus for class. I was even invited to speak about networking at NAFE (the National Association of Female Executives.) At this point, I recognized myself as a younger version of my mother.

After three and a half years in New Mexico, my parents encouraged me to transfer to Emerson College in Boston. I attended class in the morning, interned at a public relations firm in the afternoon and then walked to my job selling cellular phones at the Prudential Center at night. The public relations firm was a small boutique agency on Newbury Street owned by two Boston University graduates. They taught me everything about public relations, taking me on photo shoots, television interviews and client events. Their red pens marked up all of my press releases until they were acceptable. When my internship was over, they hired me as a part-time associate. I was thrilled to have the chance to learn even more. The skills they taught me were incredibly valuable. This is one of three internships I had in college, all of which advanced my learning and ultimately affected my career.

Upon graduation, the College approached me with a chance to attend graduate school at their new European campus in Belgium. My parents were supportive, as usual. Since they had paid for my undergraduate education, they told me I needed to take out my own loan to pay for graduate school. I applied to be a Resident Director and was chosen out of 100 applicants. I enjoyed working with the U.S. Embassy to promote the College, creating a student manual and leading student tours. For extra money, I taught English to some lawyers, conducted telemarketing phone calls for a European tire company and typed the Director's dissertation. On a day trip to Paris, my mentor in Belgium suggested a career in higher education and earning a doctoral degree. I ended up integrating my background and my public relations skills to promote colleges & universities.

After graduation from my master's degree, I returned to the States and helped my mom with her business while looking for a job. I was dating my future husband, who lived in South Florida. Soon after, I moved to Florida and began working as a marketing manager for the graduate school of education at a large university. Eventually I enrolled in a doctoral program at the same school where I also taught courses. After dating for a year, my boyfriend proposed on a snowmobile during a California ski trip. We were engaged for a year, and then we had a big wedding in Miami Beach in 1999 and a wonderful surprise honeymoon in Tahiti. Life was going well. We were traveling extensively and I was offered a position leading the international programs at the Law School. My job involved arranging internships and programs for law students in Costa Rica and England, where I would travel for meetings. On the weekends the University sent me to Jamaica to teach public speaking. I was a healthy, happy newlywed in my late 20s. Out of the blue, and for no particular reason, I decided to have a physical exam. The doctor asked if I would mind if a medical student could be present. As the doctor checked my neck, he asked the resident to do the same; several times. Then, the doctor looked at me and said that I should have a CAT scan of my neck taken immediately. I didn't understand why. A week later I was diagnosed with cancer. The specialist told me and my husband not to worry because thyroid cancer is a good cancer to have. "If you are going to have cancer this is the one you want." WHAT? I didn't want ANY cancer. My healthy lifestyle was not one that anyone would *ever* think that a cancer diagnosis would be in the story. I went to the gym every day, had been a vegetarian for many years and had no symptoms... now I have *cancer*?

The process of surgery, radiation and recovery was a journey. During surgery my thyroid was removed and malignant thyroid tissue was scraped off near my laryngeal nerve. Having a sore throat and weak voice are common following a thyroidectomy. So when I woke up with these symptoms, the doctors assured me that these would pass and I would fully recover. I could barely speak and finally learned that my left vocal cord had been paralyzed in the surgery. I tried Chinese medicine and speech therapy but nothing worked. I was a public speaking professor who couldn't speak???? When at a restaurant my husband had to order for me since waiters couldn't hear me. On an automated phone call, I couldn't speak my responses. This lasted for one year. Finally I traveled to New York City for reparative voice surgery (laryngoplasty) with a world-renowned specialist. During the surgery I was awake while the doctor placed a piece of silicone under my paralyzed vocal cord. My voice was tested and tuned until the physician was satisfied. For ten days following the surgery, I wasn't allowed to speak at all. My mother-in-law bought me an Etch-a-Sketch so I could communicate while staying at an upper-East side apartment of a family friend. Following the recovery period, my voice was about 90% back to the original strength.

Seeking local support throughout my cancer experience, I couldn't find any. So, I began the ThyCa of South Florida - the

Thyroid Cancer Survivor's Association using my marketing and PR skills to launch the group and attract members. We met at a local hospital one Saturday each month. I led the meetings and had guest speakers and new members often. After having children another amazing survivor took over the meetings for me. My chapter has grown over the years and now there are four ThyCa groups serving South Florida, including a bilingual one in Miami. I continue to respond to phone calls and emails for newly diagnosed patients who need someone to talk to.

Once I was feeling better, I wanted to accomplish something new, so I captained a cycling team at the University and began training with a close girlfriend for a 150 mile bike ride - the MS150. The funds raised went to the National MS Society. I had never ridden more than 20 miles on a bike. For my first training ride, I showed up on my mountain bike, which was not the right bike to be on for such a ride and could barely keep up with the group. By the date of the event, I was able to complete the ride, with a proper road bike, of course, feeling a sense of accomplishment. I knew that cancer wasn't going to hold me back! When the bike ride took place I was about 6 weeks pregnant but I didn't tell anyone. I kept it to myself because the year had just ended following my radiation therapy and the doctors recommended that I wait at least that long.

The following week, I met my parents and brother in New York City for Bike New York, an event where you bike all 5 boroughs. Before the ride, I presented my mom with a photo frame with a copy of my ultrasound announcing her first grandchild. Mom went home, while the rest of us went to the starting point. We began the ride at the World Trade

Center, traversed Manhattan and rode through Central Park. With thousands of bikes on the road, riders didn't have much space to navigate. My brother was riding close by me. Somehow, we managed to crash into each other. We landed in a NYC emergency room next to gunshot victims. What a way to spend the afternoon. My brother had a sprained arm and I didn't have any noticeable injuries. The three of us spent the remainder of the day looking for our bikes, which we could not locate and assumed were stolen. We ended our eventful day in New York City at the world famous Carnegie Deli.

The next day, my mom drove me to the airport. In the car, I wasn't feeling well. Since my mom had several unsuccessful pregnancies, I had the sense that she knew something was wrong. As I waited alone at the gate for my flight I began feeling worse. I called my doctor in Florida, who told me he could meet me at the hospital when I landed. The flight was torture. Having a miscarriage alone at 10,000 feet is not something I would recommend! The pain was unbearable. My husband met me at the plane with a wheelchair in Fort Lauderdale and we went straight to the ER. My first pregnancy was over.

A few months later I was able to become pregnant again with our first son. Interestingly enough, I was already signed up for a course to get my motorcycle license before I became pregnant. My husband and I often went on motorcycle trips in the Carolinas and California. It made sense for me to learn how to drive a motorcycle. So of course, I didn't tell them I was 5 weeks pregnant. I had been wanting to get my license, so I decided to move forward. Other than feeling a bit queasy, I passed and earned my motorcycle license. Another goal accomplished!

At the time, I was a full-time professor. Since I didn't qualify for maternity leave, I was grading papers while I was in labor before leaving for the hospital. I brought my newborn, strapped to me, when I had to attend on campus meetings. Finally, feeling torn between dealing with students or caring for my newborn, I resigned.

When my son was about 9 months old I captained a team for the Susan G. Komen Race for the Cure. My son had a good time in the jogging stroller, so I signed up again for the following year. At our son's first birthday party I wanted to announce that I was pregnant, which is exactly what happened. Our second son was born the same year.

My youngest son was two years old when I felt myself being called to do some type of work in addition to the occasional classes I taught online. I began applying my public relations skills as a consultant for my own clients and a for PR firm in West Palm Beach.

When a 100 year old business college from Massachusetts was seeking a Director for their new Palm Beach campus, I jumped at the chance, and was hired for the position. When that campus was closed two years later, after a change in administration, I continued to teach online for the College I was grateful to be able to once again work at home, where I could spend more time with the boys and play some tennis.

In 2012, another life-changing event occurred when I attended Jack Canfield's *Breakthrough to Success* seminar. My mother had attended and completed Canfield's Train the Trainer program. She wanted me to attend. At first I said I couldn't go to Arizona for 8 days. Then, when she offered to watch my sons, I agreed to take the opportunity. For the first time since I got married, I was alone, without my husband, kids or the family dog, for over a week. This time provided me the opportunity to focus on my goals and to meet amazing people from all over the world. I had an epiphany that I was no longer experiencing the personal fulfillment I once had by teaching college courses online. I needed to make a change. When I returned home, I enrolled in a professional coaching program at the University of Miami. I became a Certified Professional Coach and am working toward becoming an ACC level coach through the ICF (International Coaching Federation).

I have now returned to my entrepreneurial roots. I am teaching women how to network with confidence through my company, Think Forward Coaching Inc. I also lead the Palm Beach chapter of the Women's Prosperity Network which was just launched in November 2013. My experience of getting away when I went to the Jack Canfield Seminar, even though the days were packed with info and exercises, still it left me feeling renewed and inspired. Wanting to share that feeling with others, I recently launched *Weekend Getaways for Women Inc.,* a retreat business I created to provide women a weekend to relax and focus on their goals. These getaway retreats are offered in Florida, Connecticut and Costa Rica. My mom attended and presented at my first retreat. Having the woman who taught me about entrepreneurship throughout my life presenting at my first event was not only enlightening for the attendees; I also felt fulfilled and accomplished. I'm sure she was proud. We plan to continue to collaborate together on more projects.

Becoming an entrepreneur has helped to create a flexible schedule so I can spend time with my family. It also gives me the opportunity to spend time with other women who are on a similar life path. I play tennis as much as possible and was even captain of my team. Life is always about creating a careful balance. With persistence and perseverance, women have the power to create the reality they choose. A strong role model such as a mentor, professor or parent can empower a woman to succeed! We also learn so much from the women we spend time with on a regular basis. My family, friends, book club, classmates and colleagues have all supported me along my journey. I encourage you to choose people who are supportive, goal oriented, and who somehow use their knowledge, gifts and talents to improve the lives of others.

About the Author

Dr. Marla Friedman teaches female entrepreneurs how to use networking skills to increase their net worth. She uses proven techniques from her experience as the director of BNI (Business Network International) in New Mexico. Dr. Friedman taught MBA students how to communicate for over 15 years. She earned a doctorate in leadership and graduated from Emerson College in Boston, MA and Brussels, Belgium.

Dr. Friedman coaches women who want to be more effective networkers at Think Forward Coaching, Inc. She also offers retreats for successful women in Florida, Connecticut and Costa Rica as the founder of Weekend Getaways for Women, Inc.

Dr. Friedman was trained by Dr. Stephen Covey and Jack Canfield. She holds a Certificate of Professional Coaching from the University of Miami and is a member of the International Coaching Federation. Dr. Friedman leads the Palm Beach chapter of WPN (Women's Prosperity Network.)

Connect with Dr Marla Friedman at
marla@thinkforwardcoaching.com

Finding Your Purpose and Your Passion

Nancy Matthews

By all traditional standards of success, I had it made. My business, a full service title company, mortgage business, and real estate investment company, was thriving. The money was flowing and I was working hard and playing hard. I was taking vacations with my family, owned a beautiful home, and drove a hot red convertible. I was providing a wonderful lifestyle for myself and my two children as a single parent, and creating a great place to work for my employees (who also happened to be family members). Business was booming with opportunities to continue to grow and expand.

It looked like I had arrived. I did all of the things I was "supposed" to do to achieve success and had, by all accounts, achieved it. Why then was there still an emptiness inside me? Why then, did I feel there was something more?

I was a millionaire on paper, but my soul was bankrupt. I had become complacent and began to feel a slow death burning inside of me. The things that once gave me joy and fulfillment no longer served me. Something deep inside was calling me to dare to be different, but how could I stop doing what I was doing? This was all I knew! I was great at it and it was the source of income supporting myself, my family, and my employees. I wanted to call it quits, close up my businesses, move out of state, and get a fresh start. I wrestled with my desire to break out and do something different, and struggled with the guilt I felt that by doing so would cause extreme hardship for my employees (who remember, were also my family).

It was in this place of internal struggle and complacency that the search for finding MY purpose and passion began. I read books, attended seminars, listened to CD's, and continued searching. By opening myself up to new possibilities and connecting with like-spirited people, opportunities to express myself and create a business that would provide more personal fulfillment appeared. The more I explored and searched for the answer to, "What's next?" the more easily those answers appeared.

My first logical answer to the question "What's Next?" was to dovetail my existing business and experience with something new, but similar. Having great success and extensive knowledge in real estate investing, I developed a seminar program to share my "Foreclosure Secrets" with other investors who wanted to create financial freedom through real estate. This new venture brought more excitement and enthusiasm into my life and at first I felt I had found "the answer." The problem was I wasn't very good at speaking in public. Fortunately, my sister, Trish Carr, is a public speaking expert (and also a successful real estate investor), and she showed me how to get in front of the room without my knees knocking, throat closing, and palms sweating.

Trish and I became partners in the Foreclosure Secrets program and were building that business, sharing our secrets with others so they, too, could experience the financial rewards that real estate investing can provide. As a firm believer in always improving my skills and craft, I attended an event called "Seminar Bootcamp." It was there that my next turning point on the path to finding my purpose and passion occurred, and the unfolding of what has now become my mission and my "WHY" was born.

The instructor, Tony Martinez, surveyed the room of 80 people who were aspiring or already successful speakers and he noticed that only 15% of the room was women. He said, "We need more female speakers, women leaders, and women who act like women, not women acting like men. Who in this room is willing to step up to the plate, to take action, and be the forerunner and example for women to be leaders in their own right, not women trying to be men?" In that instant I felt something deep inside of me stir. It was like an electric shock to my system and I jumped out of my seat and shouted, "Me, Me, Me!" His call to action hit a chord inside of me that I didn't even know existed. Until that moment I didn't know how important it was to me to take a stand for women's empowerment. In retrospect, I now see that it is something I've always stood for, believed in, and acted upon. I just didn't recognize that I was doing it.

The significance of this event is not that I am now the Founder of Women's Prosperity Network, a global community impacting thousands of women worldwide, or that I am a leading business consultant, author and sought after speaker. The significance is in the spark that was ignited in that moment that created the space for the continuous unfolding and fulfillment of my personal mission. The chord that was hit when Tony spoke from the front of the room was the chord of "What's Next?" and set me on the path of looking inside myself instead of outside to find my purpose, my passion, and my personal power.

Finding your passion and your purpose is a journey, not a destination. Through different times and phases of my life my purpose has changed, and I know it will continue to grow and evolve. I remain open to this exciting evolution and have learned to trust my intuition to guide me on the journey.

To learn more about trusting your intuition, enjoy my free gift audio download *"How to Realize, Trust and Follow Your Intuition"* at NancyMatthews.com/intuition

Since you're reading this book, there are a few things I know (or think I know) about you:

- You are also on a journey of self-discovery, empowerment and personal fulfillment.

- You are willing to invest in yourself to explore and experience the life of your dreams.

- Your dreams are "Big Dreams" that go beyond material passions.

- You are committed to making a difference, not only for yourself, but in the lives of others as well.

- You are a "Visionary with Guts!" A heart-centered and passionate person who has a vision and the guts to go for it.

I have been dubbed "The Visionary with Guts" and I know that within each and every one of us is a visionary and that the "guts" comes from having people to support, encourage, and guide us in fulfilling our vision.

The "guts" comes from being willing to face the obstacles and challenges which will no doubt surface, and move beyond them with the conviction and commitment to fulfilling your vision.

The "guts" comes from being willing to look inside yourself to find your purpose and your passion, and knowing that success is a journey, not a destination.

I offer you the following *7 Simple Steps to Reveal Your Passion, Purpose & Power*. These are the steps that I used (and continue to use) to reveal my passion and purpose. I invite you to be patient with the process, to remain open and aware, and to listen for those moments, those turning points which occur that ignite the spark within you that touches upon your true purpose, passion, and personal power.

7 Secrets to Revealing Your Passion & Purpose

Secret 1 – RESERVE TIME FOR YOURSELF

It all starts with YOU. Reserve time for yourself. Give yourself permission to spend at least 15 minutes each day just for you (30 minutes would be even better). You'll be best served by beginning your day with this 15 minute 'me' time (although any time is better than no time.)

Secret 2 - HAVE AN "INSIGHTS" NOTEBOOK

Get a journal, notepad, or even one of those old-fashioned black and white composition books. This is where you will start to write down your notes, ideas, insights, thoughts, and dreams. Not a writer? No worries. The exercises we suggest are easy and don't require you to be a literary genius. If you can write a "To Do" list or jot down ideas on a post-it note, you can do these exercises.

Secret 3 - RECOGNIZE WHAT MAKES YOU HAPPY

As you go through your day, start to recognize those times when you're feeling happy and notice what you are doing at those times. Write down in your notebook the things you do that make you happy. This list will grow over time. Just be sure to capture at least one thing each day that makes you happy. It could be as simple as giving (or getting) hugs, taking a long hot shower, singing songs along with the radio, walking the dog, etc.

Secret 4 - SCHEDULE "HAPPY TIME"

Be sure that you schedule "happy" time in your day and your life. From the things you discovered in Secret 3, make time to do at least one of those things each day. Using this simple step, you'll be living a happier life.

Secret 5 - IDENTIFY YOUR HEART'S "SOFT SPOT"

This is the beginning to revealing your true passion and purpose. Answer this question, "If all my financial needs were met, my S.E.X. needs (Safety, Essentials and Xtras) were covered, and I had so much money that I had to give some away, who would I give it to and why?" Another way to look for this is to determine where is your heart's soft spot? Do you want to help children? Women? Animals? Taking the time to look at what you would do for others if you weren't so busy taking care of the basic needs for yourself and your family, will allow your passion to be exposed.

Secret 6 - GET SPECIFIC, LIST THE DETAILS

Now it's time to get specific. Think again about your soft spot. Who do you want to help or serve? What are some of the ways that you can help them? For example, a person who wants to help women who are victims of domestic violence may want to start a shelter for them, to develop programs to help them get out of their situation and start a new life. What is your heart's soft spot? Where do you think there's a need to be filled and what can YOU do to help fill the need? This is when you will not only state what it is that you want to do to help others (as you did in #5 above), you will also list the details of what you need to do to make it happen.

Remember that revealing your passion and purpose is a process and it will likely take some time. Be patient and kind to yourself, but be persistent. Do Not Give Up! To have your dreams and goals come to fruition you must keep your focus on them consistently.

Secret 7 - WRITE IT DOWN AND SAY IT OUT LOUD 7 TIMES A DAY

Once your passion and your purpose are revealed to you, write it down on a piece of paper. Then make 3 copies and put them clearly where you'll see them on a regular basis. On the bathroom mirror, on the refrigerator, on the dashboard of your car – wherever you'll see it often throughout the day. Read it regularly, at least 7 times per day. Thoughts become things! The more you think it, say it, and believe it, the more it will come to you.

Bonus – Secret 8 – BE OPEN AND ALERT

Keep your eyes, ears, and mind open. Now that you have identified, stated, and affirmed your passion and purpose, opportunities to fulfill your heart's desire will appear. I'm sure you can remember a time that you wanted a red car, bought a red car, and then suddenly more and more cars on the road were just like the red car you just purchased. Did it happen that lots of other people wanted the same car at the same time you did? Or was it just that once your red car was identified to you, it became part of your thinking and visual awareness? You've identified your passion and your purpose (just like you did with the red car). Be alert. Pay attention to what you hear on the radio, TV, new people you meet, conversations, magazines, and in other media.

Fulfilling your passion and purpose will happen. It is truly magical and it is your life's purpose to fulfill your mission. Remember, you are a "Visionary with Guts!"

About the Author

Nancy Matthews is known as *The Visionary with Guts* for her perseverance and commitment in overcoming obstacles, challenges and distractions in achieving her goals. She teaches the mindset and marketing strategies that allowed her to grow from a mixed up little girl from Brooklyn, a struggling single mom living paycheck to paycheck, into a successful business owner, proud parent, respected leader and sought after speaker.

Author of *The One Philosophy*, *Visionaries with Guts* and creator of the highly acclaimed "Receiving Your Riches" course, Nancy has been featured several times on NBC and The John Tesh Radio Network, and has shared the stage with some of today's leading experts on business and transformation.

As founder of Women's Prosperity Network (WPNGlobal.com), Talk Show Host, Speaker and Master Coach, Nancy works with individuals and organizations to support them in bringing their visions to life.

Contact: Nancy@NancyMatthews.com
http://nancymatthews.com/

Made in the USA
Charleston, SC
09 March 2014